MOVING TO ST. PETERSBURG

THE UN-TOURIST GUIDE

CINDY DOBYNS

Dedicated to my Mom, who is the nicest person on the planet and deserves to live in utter bliss.

CONTENTS

FOREWORD

BY RICK BAKER, MAYOR OF ST. PETERSBURG, 2001-2010 AND PRESIDENT OF THE EDWARDS GROUP

Welcome to Cool St. Pete!

Welcome to St. Petersburg, a sunny town with a cool vibe. The Burg is the 4th largest of Florida's 400 cities and is in the Southeast's 2nd largest television market. It is also quite simply one of the best cities in America to work, live, play, create, study, pedal and visit!

- WORK St. Pete is home to many large 1000+ employers in finance, technology, entertainment, defense, and biotech manufacturing and others employing a young and talented workforce:

  - Home Shopping Network (world headquarters)

  - Raymond James Financial (world headquarters)

  - Jabil (world headquarters - electronics - Fortune 200)

  - Tech Data (world headquarters - computer/electronics - Fortune 200)

  - General Dynamics (world headquarters - defense - Fortune 100)

- Cox Media (world headquarters – Valpak)

- Duke Energy, Honeywell Aerospace, Franklin/Templeton, and more

- LIVE Throughout the city are beautiful neighborhoods with parks, playgrounds (including Florida's largest playground at Dell Holmes Park), public pools, dog parks, athletic fields, skateboard parks and a great quality of life. Downtown has become a large, growing neighborhood with thousands of people living in condos, apartments and townhomes, in addition to being the center of business and government. Close to 1,000 rental apartment units are now under construction downtown. St. Pete is also America's first designated "Green City," a robust evaluation that affirms our commitment to the environment and our natural resources.

- PLAY St Pete's downtown is the gathering place for young professionals from the entire St. Pete/Tampa area. No other major city downtown in Florida matches St. Pete's nighttime vibrancy. Sidewalk restaurants and cafés line our streets downtown – also home of MLB's Rays (baseball), NASL's Rowdies (soccer), the Firestone Grand Prix of St. Pete (IndyCar) and 400 annual waterfront events from music and food festivals to the largest weekly outdoor farmers and craft market in the Southeastern U.S.

- CREATE St. Petersburg is a center for culture with several downtown museums including the internationally renowned Dali Museum, Chihuly Collection, Museum of Fine Arts, three downtown performing arts centers, many galleries, performing arts companies, significant arts education programs, and an entire Warehouse Arts District home to glass, ceramics, photographic and other visual artists - St. Petersburg has consistently been named America's #1 Arts City for cities under 500,000 people.[1]

City of St. Petersburg

- STUDY   Tens of thousands of students study at the University of South Florida St. Petersburg, Eckerd College, Stetson University College of Law and St. Petersburg College. Draper Laboratory (formerly of MIT), Johns Hopkins - All Children's Hospital (teaching hospital), SRI International (formerly Stanford Research Institute), NOAA, USGS, International Ocean Institute, Coast Guard Sector St. Petersburg (Florida's west coast headquarters) and the many members of the St. Petersburg Ocean Team anchor downtown's University-Marine-Medical sector.

- PEDAL   St. Pete is one of America's top 10 bicycle cities (St. Pete is with Austin, Portland, Minneapolis, Denver, Chicago, New York City, Boston, San Francisco - America's cool cities). Grab a CityTrails map and pedal from downtown to Tarpon Springs, or anywhere else you want to go.

City of St. Petersburg

- VISIT St. Petersburg/Pinellas is one of Florida's major tourist destinations attracting 5.5 million overnight visitors in 2012 spending more than $7.2 billion; visitors included more than 1 million from Europe and Latin America. St. Petersburg area beaches have consistently been named at the top of the nation's best beaches lists – including Dr. Beach, USA Today, TripAdvisor, Parents Magazine and Peter Greenberg – St. Pete's Ft. Desoto Park North Beach was ranked #1 in the nation in 2005.

As Mayor of the 'Burg from 2001-2010, you would expect me to love the city, but I am not alone. *The New York Times* recently named St. Petersburg one of the 52 places to go in 2014 in the world – only eight cities in America appear on the list. So, welcome to Cool St. Pete! We have a saying here that *"Every day is another great day in St. Petersburg!"* It won't be long until you will be saying that, too.

[1] Source: www.city-data.com/top1.html

INTRODUCTION

LOTS OF BUZZ ABOUT A WONDERFUL WATERFRONT LIFESTYLE

Sprawling out into the Gulf of Mexico on Florida's West Coast is St. Petersburg, connected by land only north to Clearwater and surrounded by water everywhere else. It makes for an impressive arrival as you take in the view from the highest span of the spectacular Sunshine Skyway, named one of the World's Top 10 Bridges by The Travel Channel or drive on bridges from Tampa that seem to barely skim the waves.

Long ago known as a place where people from the Midwest came to retire, St. Petersburg and its lively beaches have evolved to a vibrant, artistic, and fun place to live, work, study and retire. In fact, Lonely Planet calls it "Tampa's more arty and youthful sibling..." Most recently, Tampa Bay Business Journal reported that St. Petersburg has been named to *Money* magazine's list of Best Places to Retire.

"The city was praised along with nine other U.S. cities for being affordable, offering access to cultural events, beaches and other activities in addition to close proximity to world-class health care."

Downtown St. Petersburg has experienced an astonishing makeover that turned sleepy streets into colorful avenues of bustling outdoor cafes and new restaurants, boutique hotels, art galleries and storefronts under residential lofts and alongside condominium towers with waterfront views.

From charming beach communities of low-rise condominiums and townhomes, to single-family homes lining canals, to lakefront multi-family developments, St. Petersburg has plenty of waterfront land to enjoy. Residents love unlimited beach access, lots of boat launches, fishing docks, and lush spacious parks (count 'em—over 150) that have been designated to remain parks, even those along the valuable waterfront. High fives to members of the Garden Club of St. Petersburg who work their green thumbs to keep St. Petersburg beautiful, fulfilling the club's mission from the year 1928 still today: *"The protection of the beauty given us by nature and creation of new beauty is a noble aim for any organization. We ask your cooperation in fulfilling our aims for St. Petersburg."* In 1961 the City of St. Petersburg formed the City Beautiful Commission to assist and promote the beautification of St. Petersburg and it shows.

St. Petersburg offers a slower pace than most metropolitan cities of comparable size, yet plenty of outdoor activities, including professional spectator sports and plenty of cultural offerings so you can be as busy or relaxed as you want to be. Roads are wider and less congested making for a pleasant Sunday afternoon drive. Full-time residents numbering about 250,000 are friendly and eager to serve. The city originated as a resort destination and that environment of southern hospitality continues today. Unlike resort cities that grow solely to support an attraction, this one has been around for a long time with established business owners who have built relationships with generations of customers.

Combine smiling faces with sun and water and you, too, will blossom in St. Pete, also affectionately known as The Burg.

Reason #1
Low Cost of Living

Start with the happy fact that you no longer need winter coats, boots, scarves, and mittens. Keep smiling when you learn that residential monthly electric bills will be surprisingly lower, even if you factor in the warmer summer months. Florida has no state income tax, property taxes are much lower, and home prices are less for comparable living space, compared to most areas of the country. With all the sunshine, you can even grow some of your own produce at home, shaving hundreds off the annual grocery bill. Or visit downtown St. Petersburg's Saturday Morning Market for fruit and veggies fresh from the farm and more.

Reason #2
Dolphins in Your Backyard

If you've always dreamed of a waterfront home, you will find everything from charming beach cottages, towering condominiums with balcony views, custom-built mansions, contemporary single-family homes along canals, as well as villas, carriage and town homes in gated, master-planned communities with lakes stocked with fish. According to the United States Census Bureau, the city has a total area of 137.6 square miles (356.4 km^2). 61.7 square miles (159.9 km^2) of it is land, and 75.9 square miles (196.5 km^2) of it or 55.13 percent is water. Rest assured, wherever you live will be near water. Where else can you find dolphins in your backyard?

Visit St. Pete Clearwater

Reason #3
Accessible Beaches

Growing up across the street from the Gulf of Mexico, I did not truly appreciate Treasure Island beach. Sometimes we need to go away and come back to realize the value of what we had. Even after a career that included travel to Caribbean islands, The Bahamas, and Ocean City, my vote for the city with the best and most accessible beaches is still St. Petersburg, hands down. Joint efforts on the part of Pinellas County, the State of Florida, our local beach municipalities and citizen volunteers employed in our dune replanting make you realize how important the beaches are to local residents, as well as tourists. St. Petersburg is one of the few destinations where you can see both sunrise and sunset. And until you've seen the famous green flash from any of the beaches of St. Petersburg, your bucket list is not complete.

Visit St. Pete Clearwater

Reason #4
Excellent Healthcare

Pediatricians actually outnumber gerontologists here—so much for the stereotype as a city for old people. HCA's West Florida Division is the largest healthcare system in the Tampa Bay area. Emergency room wait times below the national average are posted on hospital websites, billboards and by texting "ER" to 23000—what technology! A total of 10 hospitals in St. Petersburg are served by a network of medical specialists throughout Pinellas County. And nearby Tampa General Hospital and Moffitt Cancer Center rank number one and two respectively in the area. [1] Three of the hospitals are acute care centers and the award-winning All Children's Hospital, a Johns Hopkins Medicine facility, treats critically ill children from all over the state of Florida.

[1]U.S. News and World Report's Best Hospital Survey 2012-13

Reason #5
Midwestern Friendliness

"Only in St. Pete" is a frequent refrain here. We roll our eyes when traffic stops on 66th Street to allow a mother duck and her ducklings to cross the six-lane road. Turtles and tortoises are gently turned around when they wander into dangerous territory. Dog friendly beaches and parks can be found here. Travelocity lists 60 pet-friendly hotels where the whole family can stay as you relocate. More than 100 neighborhoods throughout St. Petersburg are populated by kind, generous humans who rally for local causes, support each other, and exhibit pride in their pet-friendly "Burg."

Reason #6
Unlimited Outdoor Activities

City of St. Petersburg

If you are seeking opportunities to spend more time outdoors, you will love the Florida lifestyle in St. Petersburg. Our area is a sporting paradise for participants and spectators alike. St. Pete is the home of major league baseball's Tampa Bay Rays and a Guinness World Record sanctioned autographed baseball collection that has been named Little Cooperstown. Every year, downtown becomes a raceway for the Firestone Grand Prix. Play tennis or golf, go biking and birding. Or indulge your favorite water sports in the Gulf of Mexico, Tampa Bay or numerous lakes. Sunken Gardens is now a century old collection of Florida's botanical best. Walk through Roser Park, an outdoor museum dedicated to the historic district. Nearly every community offers a recreation area, and, if not, you can go to one of 150 county parks where children's playgrounds, ball fields, racquetball courts, bicycle and walking trails abound. Even the shuffleboard courts here have achieved international renown.

Reason #7
Year-Round Fruit and Flowers

St. Pete is quite simply, pretty, with tree-lined streets, flowering bushes, and green lawns. Thanks to wise city leaders in the 1970s, reclaimed water is used for irrigation to keep everything lush. Northerners will admittedly miss the marked change of seasons, but it won't be long before you appreciate brilliant red Royal Poinciana, purple Jacaranda, and yellow Tabebuia trees, wafting scents from jasmine and orange blossoms, fresh aloe and surprising night-blooming cactus. Winter here brings bright impatiens, bougainvillea, hibiscus and begonias in a variety of colors. Neighbors welcome help harvesting grapefruit, mangoes, oranges, and avocados. Soon you'll be stringing holiday lights on palm fronds, too.

Reason #8
Entertainment and Attractions

Hop on a trolley, ferry, helicopter, or Segway to tour downtown St. Pete during the day. At night, discover jazz clubs, beach bars, and restaurants with an array of talented musicians who continue to play after hours so diners can dance off their meals. You'll find ballroom dancing, stand-up comedy, and poetry readings, or head to Gulfport Casino (though deceptively named) for swing and salsa dance events. No less than nine festivals take place here annually, notably the EATS festival downtown and Bands on the Sand each Memorial Day in Treasure Island, providing plenty of wide beach to stretch out and watch the world go by. You might even have a chance to *be* the entertainment since this area's Film Commission attracts lots of film crews that need extras. Keep a watchful eye for celebrities. St. Pete/Clearwater has been the location for such films as ***Dolphin Tales 1 and 2, Six Dance Lessons in Six Weeks, The Investigator, Sunlight Jr., Spring Breakers,*** and ***Magic Mike.***

Visit St. Pete Clearwater

Reason #9
Arts, Culture and Music

St. Pete has a vibrant arts community. They open galleries, sponsor art shows, put on plays, and host special events to celebrate visual and performing arts. Several downtown venues combine with the local college theaters to offer artistic programming year round. Among an impressive list of five museums is the Dali, a unique structure that is art in itself, built to house the largest collection of Salvador Dali's work outside of Europe. For eclectic local art, experience the Old Florida feel of Gulfport and its Art Village Courtyard.

Visit St. Pete Clearwater

21

Reason #10
Wonderful Weather

St. Petersburg averages 361 days of sunshine each year. Need we say more?

CHAPTER 1

HISTORY OF THE SUNSHINE CITY

Travel destinations trying to lure visitors could learn a lot studying the history of St. Petersburg. During the Sunshine City's Golden Years in the 1920s, city leaders advertised extensively using photos of bathing beauties on the beach, giving away picture postcards to encourage visitors to write to friends and family, and launching a Festival of States Parade to honor the flags of visitors from northern states, an event that encouraged extending tourist season. Weather forecasts were flaunted on the front page of The St. Petersburg Times, comparing temperatures up north. The Evening Independent gave the newspaper away for free on days the sun didn't shine (averaging only four free issues a year!) Early pioneers of the Sunshine City were people of color who built the railroads and then settled here to run the hotels and attractions. Large numbers of tourists in the 1920s arrived by auto, railroad, and yacht. The city infrastructure grew to add more hotels and eventually houses. That's exactly what happens now, when visitors decide to make St. Pete their permanent home.

St. Petersburg began as a resort dream for Detroit investor General John Williams who bought 2,500 acres of land on Tampa Bay. Our town has thrived to become that and more. The Detroit, named for his birthplace, was St. Petersburg's first hotel and still attracts tourists to his realized vision of broad streets and graceful parks. St. Petersburg got its name from the next wealthy investor who came from St. Petersburg, Russia. Peter Demens built the Orange Belt railroad that kick-started the population growth.

Skip Milos / Tampa Bay Rays

A proud baseball city, St. Petersburg can lay claim to initiating spring training in Florida when its former mayor Al Lang lured the St. Louis Browns here in 1914.

That same year saw the birth of the commercial airline industry when pilot Tony Jannus flew the first scheduled airline flight with a passenger across Tampa Bay. Imagine that happening right here a century ago! St. Petersburg can also lay claim to being the birthplace of National Airlines, which was later absorbed by Pan Am Airways.

In 1920, the city opened a Museum of History, foretelling the need to maintain records benchmarking St. Petersburg's contributions to tourism and to commercial aviation. Today, the museum proudly features a full-size working replica of the Benoist Airboat, a timeline of the city's early days as a resort and spa destination, and Little Cooperstown, an exhibit of autographed baseballs from as early as the 1880s.

Credit C. Perry Snell, one of St. Petersburg's greatest boosters and developers, if you like the Mediterranean architecture you see in The Vinoy® Renaissance St. Petersburg Resort & Golf Club downtown, in the historic community of Snell Isle, in the homes along Coffee Pot Bayou and in the Jungle Prada neighborhood. Snell and other developers left a legacy of "Spanish Castles" throughout St. Petersburg.

Loews Don Cesar Hotel

During World War II, St. Petersburg was home for thousands of military families serving at the U.S. Coast Guard Station on Bayboro Harbor or training for the Army Air Corps. After the war, many military veterans, who hailed from farms in landlocked states, saw this as the land of opportunity and returned to marry and live here.

In 1924, Gandy Bridge was finally built, connecting St. Petersburg to Tampa, a commute that used to take six hours by car or a couple of hours on a steamship across Tampa Bay. Then in 1954, the Sunshine Skyway Bridge opened connecting St. Petersburg with South Florida, making it easier to reach the Gulf Coast cities of Sarasota and Fort Myers. Previously, people had to take a ferry or drive the long way around through Tampa to head south and connect with the Tamiami Trail, the main thoroughfare to Miami.

With the advent of air conditioning, single-family home construction thrived in the next two decades as the population grew. Subdivisions like Meadowlawn, Tyrone Gardens, Orange Hill and Orange Estates provided homes, promoted with the promise of orange trees in your front yard! Giving new homeowners the tropical environment spawned the idea of a Florida room with jalousie windows, nowadays replaced with pocket sliding glass doors and screened-in swimming pools. The city needed more housing for retirees, retail shops, and roads to accommodate vehicles. The 1960s introduced St. Petersburg's municipal marina, the main library, the Bayfront Center, and the Museum of Fine Arts.

City of St. Petersburg

The revitalization of the downtown area in the past few years attracted national retail shops, art galleries, restaurants, museums and theaters. Also drawn to the area are schools like the waterfront campus of The University of South Florida, and numerous medical facilities providing care for all ages, including All Children's Hospital and Research Center, a member of Johns Hopkins Medicine; all combine to make St. Petersburg an attractive place to live.

USF St. Petersburg

CHAPTER 2

KNOW YOUR GEOGRAPHY ABOUT ST. PETERSBURG

Here is the best tip to remember about finding your way around St. Petersburg: The streets are laid out in a grid with avenues running east and west parallel to Central Avenue and streets heading north or south. Things can get a bit tricky around the waterways and you *must* leave a trail of breadcrumbs if you venture into Venetian Isles, but once you establish your direction, driving is easy on mostly wide lanes without curbside parking. Note: That large body of water to the West is not the ocean. It is the Gulf of Mexico. The water to the East is Tampa Bay. Boca Ciega Bay is located on the north side of the mouth of Tampa Bay and is bordered by St. Petersburg, Tierra Verde, St. Pete Beach, Treasure Island, Gulfport, Seminole, and Madeira Beach. Bridges include Courtney Campbell Causeway (S.R. 60) from Clearwater to the North, the W. Howard Frankland Bridge (I-275) and Gandy Bridge (U.S. 92) heading east to Tampa and the picturesque Bob Graham Sunshine Skyway spanning four miles across Tampa Bay south through Bradenton, Sarasota and Port Charlotte all the way to Naples and Marco Island on the southern tip of Florida's Gulf Coast.

Downtown St. Petersburg is on the east shore – yes, it is a waterfront downtown, making most people's decision about whether to live downtown or on the water moot. Tropicana Field, where the Tampa Bay Rays play baseball and Albert Whitted Airport, an executive airport, can be found here, as well as shopping, dining and entertainment, museums, and art galleries.

Most of the beaches are on the west coast comprising a string of island communities that hug the mainland, starting with Fort De Soto Beach, Pass-a-Grille Beach, St. Pete Beach, Sunset Beach, Treasure Island, Madeira Beach, Redington Beach, North Redington Beach, Redington Shores, Indian Shores, Indian Rocks Beach, Belleair Beach, and Sand Key, north to Clearwater Beach.

Maximo Beach and Park, located along 34th Street and Pinellas Point Drive S. overlooks Boca Ciega Bay; it features a 10-foot observation tower, with a breathtaking view of the Sunshine Skyway Bridge and the Gulf of Mexico. The city has two white sandy public beaches, Spa Beach and North Shore Beach on the shores of Tampa Bay. Spa Beach, located at the base of the St. Petersburg Pier, once housed a toboggan slide and solarium for early tourists and residents. Egmont Key is a state preserve and island off the coast of St. Petersburg, accessible only by boat.

Pinellas County Communications

St. Petersburg, located within Pinellas County, has a population of about 250,000, making St. Petersburg the fourth largest city in the state of Florida and the largest city in Florida that is not a county seat. The County seat is in the adjacent city of Clearwater. The total population for Pinellas County is 921,319 as of 2013, but keep checking the U.S. Census, as those numbers are growing every year.

Within the center of St. Petersburg are numerous neighborhoods and commercial centers where residents work in medical, legal, retail, hospitality and other services. A mini-high technology and business corridor has formed along the northeast portion of the city as more and more northern companies realize they can operate in the sunshine more productively than in the snow when staffed by happy, stress-free employees who enjoy an easy commute to work. Something to note regarding commuting distances from Tampa to St. Petersburg and especially the beaches: You will often see Tampa/St. Pete linked together as the destination and as a newcomer, you might expect to live in one of these cities and drive to work in the other. It is approximately 40 miles from St. Petersburg Beach to Tampa, so it's a long drive, albeit a scenic one! This may not seem like much, if you've been commuting from state to state like many northern workers. We Floridians would rather spend time enjoying the sunshine and water than battling traffic. And, if you must board a plane for work each week, you will appreciate two airports. To the north is St. Petersburg-Clearwater International Airport (PIE / KPIE) a mere 13 miles from the center of the city. Only 20 miles away is Tampa International Airport (TPA / KTPA), which brings international, as well as domestic airlines to this area.

Getting Around Town

Driving is easy once you learn the grid system and install a compass on your dashboard if you are directionally challenged. Just remember the sun rises in the East and sets in the West and don't sneer at this tip...If you're moving here from any eastern coastal city, it will take a while to realize the water is the other way.

Pinellas Suncoast Transit Authority has an excellent website (www. psta.net) to plan a commute by bus to anywhere in St. Petersburg, including the beaches. Real Time bus information works with GPS technology to plan your route and provide reliable, real-time departure information when your bus is up to 30 minutes away. The beaches and downtown offer trolleys, too. Amtrak has a station at 5251 110th Avenue North in Pinellas Park Square in Clearwater, but these are not commuter trains to local destinations. You left those trains behind!

St. Petersburg is a bicyclist's best friend and in fact, the city has created a circuitous route called the Fred Marquis Trails www.pinellascounty. org/trailgd that will eventually cover a 75-mile loop through the beaches. The trails currently extend from mainland St. Petersburg to Tarpon Springs.

Pinellas County Communications

CHAPTER 3

CAN YOU LIVE WELL HERE?

Cost of Housing

Housing is inexpensive in Florida, relative to northern states and apparently you can negotiate. The median listed price for vacant houses and condos on the market for 2013 in this state: $199,900. The median sales price was $165,400. Broken down, a single-family home price in Florida is $178,100, while for a condo, it is $127,200, according to Zillow.com.[1] Homes are selling well here, but still it is a buyer's market. In fact, the median sales price for a single family home in all of Pinellas County in 2013 was $162,250 and for condos/townhomes, it was $113,000, which represents a 20 percent increase year over year. Those prices get even lower in St. Petersburg alone, not including the higher priced beach areas. The median sales price for a single family home in St. Petersburg is only $130,800. You can check the median prices for homes in the various zip codes for St. Petersburg by checking www.city-data.com/housing/houses-St.-Petersburg-Florida.html. You can also see recent home sales, real estate maps, and a home value estimator for St. Pete zip codes 33701 through 33716.

Depending on your location, though, be forewarned to check out the cost of flood insurance before signing on the dotted line.

Upscale neighborhoods like Broadwater, Causeway Isles, Historic Old Northeast, Snell Isle and the beaches have home values ranging from the mid-$400,000s to several million dollars. What a buyer is willing and able to pay for their slice of paradise is relative. Know this, however. When comparing the same square footage and amenities, you will pay less in St. Petersburg than in most cities of comparable size and population.

If you choose to rent before buying, look at condominium rentals, as well as apartment complexes. Investors who have been snapping up bargains in the last few years often rent units out, seasonally, or year round. Median gross rent in St. Petersburg, Florida in 2012 was $890. Realtor.com has a handy calculator to help you decide to rent or to buy.

Here are the average prices of various sizes and styles of housing in the St. Petersburg, Florida area.

- $180,000 - A one-bedroom condo in downtown St. Petersburg
- $109,000 - A 1940s two-bedroom home in St. Petersburg
- $500,250 - A three-bedroom home on Treasure Island with a pool
- $225,000 - A newly constructed townhome in St. Petersburg
- $400,000 - A two-bedroom waterfront condo on St. Pete Beach
- $709,000 - A three-bedroom waterfront single family home in St. Pete Beach

Source: Pinellas Realtor Association MLS

Compare this to what you can buy around the country:

- $550,000 - A one-bedroom condo in downtown Boston
- $700,000 - A 1940s two-bedroom home in Los Angeles
- $800,000 - Roughly five acres of land to build a home in Far Hills, New Jersey

- $1 million - A three-bedroom home in Washington, D.C that dates back to the eighteen hundreds

- $400,000 – A newly constructed townhome in Houston, Texas

- $300,000 – A two-bedroom condo in downtown Minneapolis

- $650,000 – A one-bedroom, one-bath condo in Long Island, New York

Utilities

Costs associated with housing, like electric, water, sewer and taxes, are also significantly cheaper in St. Petersburg than our northern counterparts. For example, the average residential monthly electric bill is $116.36 per 1,000 kWh, according to Duke Energy. Compare that with $128.40 in Michigan, $154.68 in New York, and $203.91 in California. For homes outfitted with gas furnaces and ovens, as many older neighborhoods are, TECO People's Gas charges $67.76 per 50 therms.

During the winter months, the average electric bill in St. Petersburg based on 1,000 kWh, drops to $94.62[2] per month, still lower than the national average which totals $124.31.

Water Bills

Using Pinellas County's central water system, 1,000 gallons will run you $4.78. Sewer rates are $4.57 per 1,000 gallons of volumetric rate. The base charge for water is $35.72 bi-monthly for water and sewer. If you are buying a home with lots of grass and landscaping you will need to keep watered, check first to see if you have an underground irrigation system already installed – bonus! – or if the neighborhood offers reclaimed water. Reclaimed water is treated wastewater and can be used for irrigation and other non-potable uses to extend our water supplies. The base charge for 1,000 gallons of reclaimed water drops from $4.78 to .88, so it's definitely worth researching. There are also bimonthly user fees for tapping into the reclaimed water system, but these will vary by neighborhoods depending on how the reclaimed water system was funded when installed. Reclaimed water saves an average of 40 percent of water use per household.

SW Florida Water Management District

Green thumbs will want to inquire about any restrictions on what you can plant. Some homeowner associations will dictate whether or not you can plant fruit trees or bushes of a certain height. Look into Florida-Friendly Landscaping™ which was developed by the University of Florida's Institute of Food and Agricultural Sciences. It follows a set of nine principles that can create a beautiful landscape that conserves water and protects our water resources. Homeowners can get more information about Florida-Friendly Landscaping™ by visiting WaterMatters.org/Yards. For a list of current fees for water, sewer and reclaimed water, including deposits, connection charges, backflow prevention devices, impact fees and more, visit www. pinellascounty.org/utilities/PDF/fees.pdf.

Property Tax

The Pinellas County property appraiser determines the assessed value of your home by taking into account fair market value, geographic location and how the property is used. Our taxes are paid in arrears in

Florida, meaning the estimated figure is relying on the previous year's comparables. When you buy a home in Florida, you are eligible for a $50,000 homestead exemption. Tax-Rates.org, a site that reports the median property tax rate by state and even by county, ranks Florida 18th out of the 50 states for property taxes as a percentage of the median income. Counties within each state will have higher or lower property tax rates based on a number of factors. For instance, a $250,000 house in Cuyahoga County, Ohio has a tax bill of almost $9,000. Westchester County in New York reports the highest median property tax in that state, levying an average of $9,003 yearly in property taxes. By contrast, in Florida, Miami-Dade County comes in as the highest with taxes of $2,756.

The median property tax in Pinellas County is $1,690 per year, based on a median home value of $185,700 and a median effective property tax rate of 0.91 percent of property value. For example, your property taxes on a $250,000 property valuation for your home would be $2,275,[1] without applying the basic $50,000 homestead exemption or any additional exemptions. By comparison, California's homestead exemption is only $7,000.

Programs like Save Our Homes keep yearly increases to a minimum, while additional exemptions for seniors, widows, disabled, and more can be added to the $50,000 homestead exemption. In 2008, Florida voters approved an additional $25,000 homestead exemption to be applied to the value between $50,000 and $75,000, so you will want to take advantage of your tax savings eligibility. Learn more at the Pinellas County Property Appraisers Office website at www.pcpao.org or call 727-464-3207.

Tax Tip: Honorably discharged veterans with a service-related permanent disability are exempt from paying property taxes in Florida. You must be a permanent resident of Florida and the U.S. Department of Veterans Affairs must confirm your disability.

[1] U.S. Census Bureau Tax Foundation and Florida Dept. of Revenue

A General Feeling of Safety

Fire

Pinellas County's public safety website (www.pinellascounty.org/publicsafety/default.htm) indicates that fire protection is provided by no less than 19 municipal and independent special district fire departments, assuring rapid response to all emergency fire or EMS calls, regardless of location. Additionally, the Pinellas County Fire Division staffs and trains Hazardous Materials Response and Technical Rescue teams. Safety and Emergency Services Department ensures the safety of residents and visitors to the area, handling everything from storm preparation to nuisance animal calls and consumer advocacy.

Law Enforcement

The St. Petersburg Police Department, with a crew of 545 sworn officers and 212 civilian support staff, have announced the crime rate in 2012 was the lowest in 40 years, due in part to enhanced technology and predictive policing that helps identify the 10 percent of the criminals who commit 90 percent of the crimes.

The Pinellas County Sheriff's Office has a staff of over 2,700 employees. Sheriff's deputies have countywide jurisdiction, but mainly patrol the unincorporated areas and the cities under contract with the Sheriff's Office for primary law enforcement services. Law enforcement services such as the K-9 Unit, Flight Section, and Marine Unit are available countywide. The Sheriff's Child Protection Investigation Division (CPID), another countywide program, protects abused and neglected children. The Sheriff's Office also took the lead in tracking sexual predators and offenders by dedicating a team of deputies to monitor the registration and activities of these individuals countywide.

The Sheriff's Office Youth Services section has grown to include School Resource Deputies in middle schools and high schools, and programs dealing with youthful offenders. The Sheriff's Office has forged strong community partnerships by offering citizens numerous opportunities to learn more about law enforcement and personal safety. Citizens from around the county can participate in the Sheriff's Citizens Academy, the Sheriff's Advisory Board, Neighborhood Watch, and Volunteers In Partnership (VIPs). Go to the handy list of services where you can find what you are looking for easily (www. pcsoweb.com/i-want-to/)

In the city of St. Petersburg, most communities have an effective Neighborhood Crime Watch and residents are encouraged to get involved with various community awareness programs led by local police. Police work actively with the Criminal Justice System to ensure that these individuals don't slip through the cracks in the system and continue to commit crimes in the city. The Police Department maintains a very comprehensive website that offers convenient resources for newcomers and invites community members to get involved.

Hospitals and Doctor's Offices

Finding great medical care in St. Petersburg is simpler than ever thanks to its award-winning hospitals and the numerous urgent care centers that have opened throughout the area. More than 300 family medical practitioners and 600+ specialists from neurology to podiatry are ready to heal you from head to toe and all parts in between.

All Children's Hospital

Families from all across the state of Florida and beyond travel to All Children's Hospital to find care for infants, children and teens with some of the most challenging medical problems. As a member of Johns Hopkins Medicine, the hospital participates in pediatric medical education and clinical research, giving patients and their families access to the most innovative treatments and therapies. More than half of 259 beds are devoted to intensive care level services. Newly redesigned, the hospital now has individual rooms where parents can comfortably spend the night in a healing environment.

St. Anthony's Hospital

The American Stroke Association recently awarded St. Anthony's Hospital its Get With The Guidelines-Stroke Gold Plus Performance Achievement Award, recognizing its success with stroke patients. Founded by the Franciscan Sisters of Allegany in 1931, St. Anthony's also excels in the fields of general surgery, orthopedics, cancer treatment, diabetes management and neurology. It was the first hospital in St. Petersburg to offer the cutting-edge technology of a 3D HD surgical robot and the first in the area to provide the community with digital mammography. A recently completed $30 million improvement project added a new Emergency Center and Patient Care Tower, new Heart and Breast Centers, and imaging and diagnostic equipment.

Bayfront Health

Bayfront Health St. Petersburg is a 480-bed teaching hospital in St. Petersburg and home to more than 1,800 health care professionals and 550 physicians representing a variety of specialties. In addition to accreditation by The Joint Commission, Bayfront is certified as a Level II trauma center, Level III regional perinatal intensive care center, comprehensive and primary stroke center, chest pain center, Level IV epilepsy center and certified hip and knee replacement center.

Hospital Corporation of America (HCA) manages six of the 10 hospitals in the general St. Petersburg area:

- St. Petersburg General Hospital, a robotic GYN Epicenter, one of only 28 such sites in the country and chosen for their excellence in patient outcomes, passion for teaching and technical expertise.

- Palms of Pasadena Hospital joined HCA in October 2013 and is a nationally-recognized leader for Barnett Continent Intestinal Reservoir (BCIR) surgery.

- Edward White Hospital, serving the St. Petersburg area for more than 35 years, services include an Orthopedic and Spine Center, Center for Wound Care and Hyperbaric Medicine, a

Skilled Nursing Unit, a Diagnostic and Imaging Center and a Comprehensive Rehabilitation Institute.

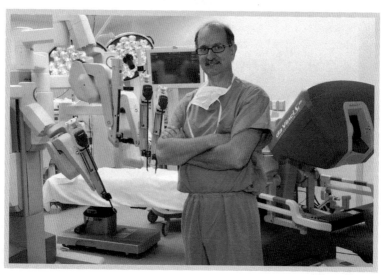

HCA Healthcare

- Northside Hospital, noted for its Cardiovascular Intensive Care Unit, featuring the latest designed and technology to facilitate recovery following cardiovascular surgery.

- Largo Medical Center is a 425-bed acute care statutory teaching hospital serving the community from two campuses – 201 14th Street SW and 2025 Indian Rocks Road South.

HCA's West Florida Division is the largest healthcare system in the Tampa Bay area and provides a complete continuum of high quality programs and services to meet the healthcare needs of residents and businesses. Four HCA Pinellas County Hospitals were recently named *Top Performers on Key Quality Measures*™ by The Joint Commission and a fifth hospital was acquired in 2013 – Palms of Pasadena.

HCA hospitals are geographically situated throughout Pinellas County and provide 4,300 people with employment. More than 1,000 of the area's most respected physicians are on the medical staffs, treating about 216,000 patients annually in emergency departments. ER wait times are posted on hospital websites, billboards and by texting "ER" to 23000.

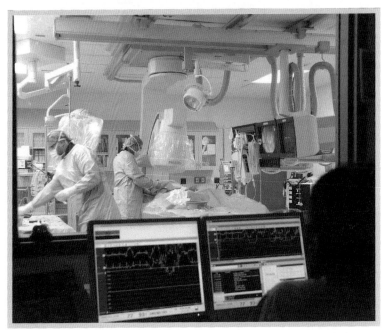

HCA Healthcare

Approximately four to five percent of all inpatient care delivered in the country today is provided by HCA facilities so chances are good that when moving to St. Petersburg or Tampa (see *Moving to Tampa: The Un-Tourist Guide*), the process of identifying medical care in keeping with your healthcare insurance will be seamless.

HCA also manages the Countryside Surgery Center, north of St. Petersburg, and these medical institutions in nearby Tampa:

Ambulatory Surgery Center of Tampa

Memorial Hospital of Tampa

Tampa Eye and Specialty Surgery Center

Town & Country Hospital

HCA Healthcare

VA Hospital

You can be overlooking the water even if you need medical care. St. Petersburg is home to one of the most beautiful and prestigious veterans administration hospitals in the country. C.W. Bill Young Department of Veterans Affairs Medical Center, located on the Intracoastal Waterway, is surrounded by the 359-acre War Memorial Park and has served the needs of our military since 1933. The hospital's area of coverage via satellite offices as far south as Naples encompasses 10 counties within Florida.

Medical Specialists

Within 25 miles of downtown St. Petersburg, you will find more than 1,000 family physicians and specialists that range from 573 pediatricians to 226 geriatric specialists. Check your insurance coverage as a guide to choosing your doctors, but you will be pleased at the wide variety of offices where you can find the care you and your family will need. Consult www.healthgrades.com for a comprehensive list.

Dentists

Here is a site to smile about: www.smilepinellas.com/Directory/index. htm. Pinellas County Dental Association maintains a website that provides an easy way to find a dentist, orthodontist, oral surgeon or other dental specialists near you.

Florida Blood Services

Give blood at one of four donor centers (now with FREE Wi-Fi) or learn where to find the bloodmobile by checking the website at www.oneblooddonor.org

Clearwater - Missouri Donor Center
1680 S. Missouri Ave
Clearwater, FL 33756
Phone: (727) 582-9500
Schedule an Appointment

St. Petersburg - 22nd Ave Donor Center
6808 22nd Ave N
St. Petersburg, FL 33710
Phone: (727) 384-4145
Schedule an Appointment

St. Petersburg - Main Donor Center
10100 Dr. MLK Jr. St. N
St. Petersburg, FL 33716
Phone: (727) 568-5433
Schedule an Appointment

Palm Harbor Donor Center
33825 US Hwy 19 N
Palm Harbor, FL 34684
Phone: (727) 568-1179
Schedule an Appointment

Hospice Care

Suncoast Hospice serves families by providing compassionate palliative care. The all volunteer Suncoast has three care centers located throughout Pinellas County and a wide network of caregivers who will travel to your home. Caregiver support groups, training classes, one-on-one counseling and more is offered to patients of any age. Suncoast Hospice presents you with another wonderful opportunity to enjoy the rewards of volunteering in the community.

Pet Care

Next to finding someone the perfect person to cut and style your hair and a new dentist that you like, identifying a veterinarian could be a challenge. Pinellas County's website makes it easier for you here (www.pinellascounty.org/animalservices/veterinary-offices.htm)

CHAPTER 4

CHOOSING WHERE IN ST. PETERSBURG TO LIVE

A Variety of Housing Choices

Housing options include:

- Townhomes, carriage homes and villas;

- Low-rises, mid-rises and high rises;

- Towering beachfront and bay front condominiums;

- Single family homes.

Gareth Rockliffe

First, decide on how much living space you will need. Then determine whether you wish to maintain a single-family home or to be part of a condo association whose fees pay for landscaping, swimming pools, insurance, and amenities particular to the community. Then, it's time to drive around and see some neighborhoods.

Take a Realtor with you to get the most information possible and to save you time looking in the wrong places based on your preferences. Ask questions about the dues associated with some neighborhoods. These reflect the care and maintenance of the area and can vary widely.

Gareth Rockliffe

As communities were developed, insightful builders took advantage of the waterways and in some cases, engaged in dredge and fill operations to ensure that every home was situated on a canal. Numerous neighborhoods nestle along Boca Ciega Bay and Tampa Bay and include boat docks in every homeowner's backyard.

If golf is more to your liking, take a look at the many housing opportunities built on golf courses where you can gaze out of your lanai to see endless manicured greens. In some golf course communities, golf membership is bundled with the home purchase. Everyone who lives there contributes to the cost of maintaining the golf club which keeps dues lower. Other communities give residents the choice of golf membership or social membership, both of which come with their share of entitlements to various amenities like a spa, community swimming pool, clubhouse, game room, theater, fitness center, etc.

If living in a metropolitan setting is your speed, St. Petersburg's downtown has received a facelift. Home buyers have fun choices like modern lofts over retail shops, historic hotel rooms converted to spacious condos, mixed use buildings with private residences above professional offices and lots of new high-rises with waterfront views. The beauty of downtown living is the ability to walk or ride a bike to convenient stores, restaurants, and other services.

Visit St. Pete Clearwater

"The City of St. Petersburg has been ranked for three years in a row as "America's #1 Arts Destinations," the best walking city in Florida, one of America's best places to retire, and home to some of the top ranked beaches in the world," says Robert Danielson, who gets to write about this wonderful city in his role leading the marketing, communications and creative services for the City.

If keeping your toes in the sand and water is key to your happy life, St. Petersburg's many interconnected beach communities beckon. Pass-a-Grille Beach on the southernmost end to Sand Key and Clearwater Beach and several islands in between hug the Gulf of Mexico shoreline of St. Petersburg and each island has its own distinct personality. Take

47

the time to visit and talk to people before choosing where you want to live. Or rent for a while first and get to know the unique areas St. Petersburg has to offer.

Should You Rent or Buy?

Only you can determine what best fits your housing needs and whether or not you plan to live in St. Petersburg long term. Realtors report that many people are buying now instead of renting because the inventory for homes and condos is low. Buyers are confident that if they had to sell quickly in order to relocate for work, they could do so. Construction of new homes, as well as apartment buildings, is on the upswing, however, so the only thing constant in the real estate industry is change.

The average rental for a two-bedroom apartment in St. Pete is $850 and more like $1,500-$2,000 for the beaches. Several new apartment buildings have gone up in downtown St. Petersburg, appealing to the young employees relocating here for jobs and seeking proximity to work. I chatted with one such new arrival who shared that he thought he would live in Tampa and commute to St. Petersburg Beach for work until he realized the distance (40 miles) and the rush hour traffic he would have to endure.

The State of the Real Estate Market

Depending on the price range, of course, you will find certain areas of St. Petersburg are seeing more activity in terms of real estate sales. Snell Isle, St. Petersburg Beach, Old Northeast, Seminole, and Pass-a-Grille Beach are selling well, especially Seminole, where the land is the highest above sea level and therefore, flood insurance is not necessary. Coldwell Banker Realtor Betty Youmans shared the profile of the typical buyers they are seeing.

"There are three kinds of customers: Families, empty nesters, and young active seniors. Some people are visitors and decide to buy and live in their homes part-time until such time as they are ready to move here permanently. They can usually find a renter in the meantime, or ask us

to make arrangements for home watch services for the months when they are away."

The kinds of questions she gets are, *"How much was the house selling for last year and how much back in 2005-06 before the housing bubble burst?"* Home prices in St. Petersburg are still a bargain. Many believe the costs were inflated prior to the years the housing bubble burst nationwide and St. Pete was no exception.

St. Petersburg has become a hip place for young people to live. That's different for those of us who have lived here forever and remember when downtown was filled with the now infamous green benches where older people would spend the day watching the world go by. The population today includes lots of young couples –schools are most important—changing the complexion of many communities.

The population on the beach is about 40 percent seasonal. It boggles the mind to walk along the beach and see so many condos—prime real estate!--buttoned down with hurricane shutters for eight months of the year.

Gareth Rockliffe

According to the Pinellas Realtor Organization's statistics as of May, 2013 the median sales price for a home in Pinellas County is $162,250. That will barely afford you a one-room, closet-sized apartment in Manhattan or a cozy two-bedroom condo in Chicago, plus you'd have to shell out an additional $30,000 for a parking spot, or a 1960s, two-bedroom ranch with about 1,000 square feet of living in Napa, California. Add big property tax rates in California, New York and New Jersey (while here they amount to approximately .91% of your home's fair market value) and moving to St. Petersburg is looking better and better.

Real Estate Services

If you have a chance to travel to St. Petersburg for vacation and decide you might want to buy, contact one of the local Realtors. The Pinellas County Realtor Organization has a good website to get you started www.pinellasrealtor.org or call (727) 347-7655. Most of the Realtors are very well connected in the City, so ask around to see who is selling successfully and actually doing this for a full-time career. During the housing bubble, *everybody* claimed to be a Realtor!

Nationwide, Realtor.com is the biggest and best resource to see the most recent inventory of homes for sale. You won't know which are under contract or already sold without the help of a Realtor. Choose carefully to find someone best suited to your needs. That shouldn't be a challenge as you will have more than 5,000 Realtors to choose from.

CHAPTER 5

SHOPPING

Grocery and Gourmet Items

When you move to Florida, you will discover Publix Supermarkets where their advertising claims "Shopping is a Pleasure." Frankly, this is one of those times when the ads are totally accurate. You will love to shop at one of 30 Publix locations throughout Pinellas County. Some are Super Stores with seafood markets, butcher shops, and liquor stores, but all have a pharmacy, deli, and bakery with the best birthday cakes in my humble hungry opinion. Busy shoppers appreciate the grocer's Aprons Program where someone near the store entrance is always preparing quick weeknight recipes with heavenly aromas or on occasion, hosting cooking classes with renowned chefs.

Winn-Dixie grocery stores are known for their outstanding beef products and you will find more than a dozen throughout the area with a good rewards program to save money on purchases.

Two locations of The Fresh Market in Northeast St. Petersburg and Clearwater are clearly not enough if you are looking for an upscale purveyor of organic foods that support local producers, growers and fishermen. It's worth circling the parking lots to get a spot, though, for good quality produce, prepared seasonal gourmet foods, and unique items.

Specialized dietary needs can be met at health food stores like Rollin' Oats, Earth Origins, and three locations of Richard's Foodporium.

You can also arrange to have fresh organic produce delivered to your door by Daisy's Organic or St. Pete Locally Grown. In downtown St. Pete, you can sample spices at Savory Spice Shop; pastas, sauces, and olive oil at Kalamazoo Olive Company; and gourmet chocolates at Kilwin's or Sweet Diva's Chocolates.

Mazzaro's Italian Market is not to be missed, not only for its 60 wines to taste and gourmet Italian hors d'oeuvres, but yummy sandwiches and take-out, too. It's small, so don't everyone go over there at once, OK? Another spice shop, Old Pass Spice Traders, can be found in John's Pass Village in Madeira Beach.

One of the largest selections of gourmet food items can be found every Saturday in downtown St. Petersburg at the Saturday Morning Market. The parking lot of Al Lang Field, First Street and First Avenue SE, is transformed during the months of October to May, into a delicious display of 200 vendors, considered one of the largest farmers markets in Florida. Gail Eggeman carefully chooses vendors offering the best organic produce, homemade cheeses, coffee, tea, fruit and vegetable juices, ethnic foods, spices, soaps, jewelry, and more...

If you're looking for that special something for your dog or cat, be sure to visit Pawsitively Posh Pooch and Classy Cats Too on 4th Street. Plan on spending some time as you browse through everything from haute couture dresses to diamond-studded collars and leashes. Yes, for dogs and cats. I told you St. Pete is a pet-friendly city!

Vintage and Book Stores

The shop that's tops for vintage clothing is Misred Outfitters. Opened in 2010, it quickly became the area's most popular vintage boutique. Misred offers designer, vintage and one-of-a-kind clothing at below market prices.

Browse antiques and vintage holiday décor inside Paper Street Market at 9th Street and Central Avenue and be sure to ask the owners how they chose that name. You can also learn to paint here. Also downtown, you'll find the luxuriously unique Mis En Chic, Little Brooklyn Vintage and Buffalo Gal for vintage clothing, accessories, and gifts.

Downloadable books and digital libraries are popular for their convenience, but the reading experience cannot compare to spending an afternoon browsing the stacks at Haslam's Bookstore in St. Petersburg. An entire section is devoted to writers who focus on Florida and who can enlighten you about the idiosyncrasies of this State. In fact, authors like Jeff Klinkenberg have made a good living out of identifying and writing about many unique personalities who define the culture of Florida. As a *Tampa Bay Times* feature writer, he found more than a few unique people in St. Petersburg to write about. See Klinkenberg's collection. Author and historian Jon Wilson's books can also be found at Haslam's. His entertaining writing style and historic photos in "The Golden Era in St. Petersburg: Postwar Prosperity in the Sunshine City" reveal how St. Petersburg became a thriving city, paradise for nearly a quarter of a million people today.

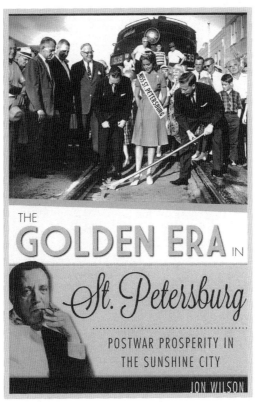

Shopping Centers

Before we get into the malls, let me just share with you St. Petersburg's unique claim to fame. Home Shopping Network's corporate headquarters, studio and broadcasting facilities are here. If you've ever succumbed to the time sensitive sales pitches on television's biggest retailer, you, too, will bow your head as you drive past the building on Roosevelt Boulevard.

St. Petersburg has one major mall, Tyrone Square Mall, on 66th Street and 22nd Avenue North where you will find a collection of the major brand retailers like Macy's, Dillards, JC Penney, and Sears along with smaller retail shops and restaurants that appeal to young shoppers. At Countryside Mall found north of Clearwater and International Mall in Tampa you will find the nationally known luxury jewelers and designer fashion stores. A few designers have opened boutiques along Beach Drive in downtown St. Petersburg as that newly chic shopping and cultural arts area has been gentrified. Take a stroll and discover some unique fashion finds.

Downtown St. Pete's newest retail, dining and entertainment destination is Sundial. The center located on 2nd Ave. North is anchored by four restaurants, including a culinary market/restaurant by renowned chefs Michael Mina and Don Pintabona. Additionally, Sundial offers a Muvico Theater, a variety of retailers for men and women and luxury spa services. The center's main attraction is a 28 foot tall sundial and life-sized frolicking dolphins. Rene Lagler, who has designed sets for an Academy Award and Grammy Awards ceremonies designed the sundial and a fountain, while Mark Aeling and St. Petersburg-based MGA Sculpture Studio created the bronze dolphins.

Personally, one of my favorite places to shop is John's Pass Village and Boardwalk located on the channel that connects the Intracoastal Waterway to the Gulf of Mexico. Located on Gulf Boulevard in Madeira Beach, one might think it is just another tourist stop, but many local residents have built their unique businesses here offering home décor, fashions, jewelry, accessories and fun gifts. Besides the great view, there's food and entertainment, too.

Fashion and Clothing in Florida

When my husband and I moved back to Florida from Virginia, my first goal was to shed the navy, black, and browns dominating my closet. I have since learned how to continue to wear those colors in lightweight fabrics and adding bright or pastel colors as accent pieces. Advice from fashion mavens Serena, age 14 and Ashley, age 11, who grew up next door, include these admonitions: *"Black is always acceptable, but wear a bright color backpack. No socks with sandals! Definitely no fanny packs. The girls also suggested learning how to achieve the layered look because the weather can change quickly and you will be going from hot outside to cold air conditioning inside. In the summer, always be prepared for rain, no matter what the weatherman says. And get a tan before you move here."*

Fashionable as my little neighbors may be, I did consult a professional, Fashion Wardrobe Stylist and owner of vStylist.com Tamy Lugo, who shares her list of *must haves* in your Florida closet:

- Two light blazers in black and in white

- Leggings

- Bermuda shorts

- White button down, white blouse, white bow tie top

- Wide Striped top

- Graphic print shirt/blouse

- Black A-line skirt

- Beige or white A-line skirt

- White pants

- Skinny/straight jeans

- Black cropped trousers

- Little black dress

- Little red dress

- Little blue dress

- Light coat

- Camis and tanks in assorted colors

- Light sweater tops in cashmere

- Light scarves in prints and assorted colors

- Nude pumps

- Animal print clutch

When asked about the rule we follow in northern climes to wear white only between Memorial and Labor Days, Tamy thankfully says that dictum no longer applies. *"Style really has no rules. It's in how you wear it. For example, wearing white during the day is OK all year long. Pair white with edgier pieces or darker hues for night time. The all-white suit can be worn in the evening only when tailored to fit seamlessly and accented by bold accessories like an outstanding pair of shoes."*

In Florida, you will want to shop for light-weight fabrics like no-cling jersey, chiffon, silk, and modal cotton. And for men? My husband reaches for a golf shirt when I tell him we need to dress up! Tamy says *"The Tommy Bahama look fits the Florida lifestyle and is a very popular style solution for men. When on an evening date, men should look for a solid color, clean cut tailored pant and shirt. Trendy studded tees or dress shirts are an option, combined with a straight leg jean or pant. Add a sporty blazer if the occasion calls for it."* Notice she did not mention a tie! Unless it's black tie or business, ties are optional here—even in many office settings.

Heavenly Heels

One of your first purchases will likely be a pair of flip flops or flat sandals, possibly exposing those toes to the elements for the very first time while making it easier to walk on the beach. (Remember to apply sunscreen to the tops of your feet.) But only wear flat sandals when the temperature stays above 74 degrees. While flip flops have undergone a fashionable makeover, now with jewels, shells, colorful fabrics and even tiny heels, Tamy cautions you to take into consideration where you'll be going.

- A wedding = no

- A casual lunch date = yes

- Running errands = yes

- Dinner at a high end restaurant = no

- Graduation = no

- Client meetings = no

"Flat sandals send a very casual, relaxed message that may not be appropriate in certain environments," says Tamy. *"If you still want comfort, try a dressy flat closed toe shoe or a two-inch wedge."* Dressy

sandals with heels are perfectly acceptable most of the time in Florida. Check out the selection at Heavenly Heels in downtown St. Pete.

Furniture and Design

If you don't already know this little secret, tuck it away for future reference —consignment stores can be the best places to shop for furniture. Think about it. Wealthy seasonal residents change their interior design décor annually, if not every season. Unique items that are barely used can be purchased for far less than the original sticker price. My girlfriend, Sue, had to drag me into one of these places because I resisted, but now I am sold, as the shop owners have sold me some of the most beautiful pieces to add to our Florida décor. Check these out:

Consignment Furniture Showroom
6130 Central Ave.
(727) 347-3982

Deja Vu Consignment Furniture
1601 34th St. N.
(727) 328-8630

Gulfport Furniture
4746 22nd Ave. S.
(727) 321-3179

Furnish Me Vintage
1246 Central Ave
(877) 557-1151

Furniture Workshop
2425 Dr. Martin Luther King Jr. St. N.
(727) 898-2013

P.A.R.C. Thrift Store
5825 66th St. N.
(727) 541-4493

Consignment Furniture
134 49th St. S.
(727) 623-4969

Buying new furniture will not be a challenge. St. Petersburg has numerous showrooms where you can browse bedroom and dining room sets, children's room furnishings, and all kinds of outdoor patio furniture. With this kind of weather, we tend to spend more of our time outdoors, so plan your budget accordingly to save room for decorating the balcony, poolside patio, or the favorite Florida room where you will do all of your entertaining. Kane's, Haverty's, Heritage House, Leader's Casual, Hudson's Furniture, and Rooms to Go will give you lots of great ideas about how to create a comfortable look for your Florida home. On-site decorators can provide invaluable tips on how to incorporate your existing furnishings. Yes, really, you don't have to convert it all to rattan. Interior designers can give you many more options that will let you keep your antiques or traditional look, adding some light, bright accessories or colors. You will find several of the furniture warehouses along 34th Street North in St. Petersburg, including American Freight, a discount furniture retailer.

Holly Dennis

As far as mattresses, there seems to be a new store opening on every corner, so bounce around to find the friendliest folks with same day delivery and pick-up of your old mattresses.

While I love to shop for furnishings, art and accessories, I find it difficult to make that final decision, unsure that I will continue to love the look when it is sitting in my living room at home. Time to call in the professionals—interior designers who will assess your lifestyle, talk with you about the kinds of things you like, and what you want to achieve with each room of the house. Devotees of feng shui will want to start this process during the construction phase if you are building a new home. I know this because I made my husband round out the corners of our driveway and entrance when we added pavers, even though it meant digging up the lawn irrigation system. It's miraculous that we're still happily married.

You have much to learn, grasshopper, about how to decorate your Florida home and several professionals in the area will be eager to help.

A list of nearly 400 interior designers in the Greater St. Petersburg area can be found on Houzz.com.

The American Institute of Interior Designers (ASID) lists hundreds of members you can consult nationwide. Many seasonal residents of Florida like to work with designers in their home states.

CHAPTER 6
WHAT TO DO AND WHERE TO GO

Arts, Culture and Music

Concerts here can be enjoyed from the balcony of your condo, sitting on a blanket on the lawn or in your boat as musical performances emanate from Vinoy Park, downtown. The annual Pops in the Park each Fall is one of several outdoor concerts that draws hundreds of people carrying picnic baskets and coolers, some setting up cozy candlelit tables for two as they share a bottle of wine and enjoy the music. Beach bars and hotels hire talented local artists to sing and play music, especially during Florida's busy tourist season, November to April. Nightly live entertainment can be found in many of the downtown restaurants and lounges, some of them literally turning the tables to become a dance club after dinner is served.

The oldest, continuously operating community theater in the state of Florida is St. Petersburg City Theatre, presenting six plays each season, plus a theater education program for children and adults.

The 2,031-seat Mahaffey Theater at the Duke Energy Center for Arts is one of Tampa Bay's top-rated performing arts venues. Home to the Florida Orchestra, it attracts the world's top artists and performances. Palladium Theater presents jazz, blues, pop and opera.

Support for the artists who call St. Petersburg home can be found in the Warehouse Arts District, "where art is made, not just shown and sold," according to their Facebook profile. It has a physical location of

First Avenue North to 10th Ave. South and 16th Street to 31st Street, but is essentially a non-profit membership organization with the goal of promoting an environment that encourages artistic work and audiences who can appreciate it. Events like a First Night Celebration or the Second Saturday Artwalk invite people to board free trolleys or drive to tour 35 warehouses, galleries and studios that stay open late that evening only.

World-renowned artist Dale Chihuly found a home for a selection of his glass sculptures courtesy of the Morean Arts Center in downtown St. Petersburg. The Chihuly Collection is breathtaking, marked by the now iconic 20-foot sculpture installed at the entrance at 400 Beach Drive. The Collection includes Chihuly's spectacular large-scale installations such as Ruby Red Icicle Chandelier created specifically for the Collection along with several popular series works including Macchia, Ikebana, Niijima Floats, Persians and Tumbleweeds..

Visit St. Pete Clearwater

A definite must-see whether you are just visiting or living here permanently, Morean Arts Center also features other artists and traveling exhibitions. Dating back to 1917 as the Art Club of St. Petersburg, Morean's galleries focus on an innovative, community-oriented approach to art and art education. A Children's Learning

Center provides a hands-on learning environment for kids of all ages and abilities.

Salvador Dali's work, too, found a home here—an exclusive home. The Dali Museum is characterized by a free-form geodesic glass bubble known as the "enigma," made of 1,062 triangular pieces of glass. It stands 75 feet at its tallest point, a 21st Century homage to the dome that adorns Dali's only other museum in his native Spain. This is an intriguing collection of 96 oil paintings and original drawings, prints, sculpture, photos, and more. You will be amazed at the visual perception created when you view the oversized piece entitled "Gala Contemplating the Mediterranean Sea" which becomes a portrait of Abraham Lincoln when you stand farther away and gaze at it.

Expansion of the Museum of Fine Arts several years ago added a new two-story building adjacent to the original structure that opened in 1965. The addition houses the special exhibition galleries, a classroom, the Interactive Education Gallery, a library, museum store, and café.

Don't miss the 100 year celebration of the birth of commercial aviation at the St. Petersburg Museum of History. An impressive display upon entering the museum talks about the first passenger aircraft that flew across the bay to Tampa, a trip that used to take hours before the bridges were built.

Speaking of commemorating history, an ambitious African American Heritage Project is underway, led by a dedicated woman named Gwen Reese who was born in one of St. Petersburg's historic African-American neighborhoods. Oral histories and walking tours will tell the story of African American's contribution building the railroads and early hotels that brought the first wave of tourists and eventually full-time residents to the region.

Topics to stimulate the scientist in the family are available at The Science and Technology Education Innovation Center located just west of Tyrone Square Mall. Students learn advanced scientific concepts thanks to classroom extension programs in conjunction with the schools and through grants. Self-guided tours of permanent exhibits during the summer months include:

Carol Samuels Observatory: The observatory features a powerful Meade 16-inch telescope. The St. Petersburg Astronomy Club, in cooperation with the Center, opens the observatory to the public throughout the year, usually on the fourth Friday of the month.

Marine Room: Featuring a **600 gallon Marine Touch Tank**, the Margaret Ewell Dickins marine exhibit includes over ten species of marine life. Visitors and students also enjoy the displays representing Florida fish and shells and learn how they interact with humans.

White Gardens and Mosaic Walk of The States: The White Gardens feature mosaics depicting the bird, flower and shape of each state in the order of its admission into the union. Stones representing each state are also part of the display. The Walk of States was created by St. Petersburg artist Attilio Puglisi.

Florida Holocaust Museum features virtual tours of this collection of works of art, photographs and historical artifacts that honor the memory of millions who suffered or died in the Holocaust. Located at 2240 Ninth Avenue South, the Dr. Carter G. Woodson African American Museum calls attention to the midtown area of St. Petersburg, which has been undergoing rejuvenation. The museum joins Mercy Hospital at the Johnnie Ruth Clarke Health Center, the Royal Theater Boys and Girls Club, and the renovated Manhattan Casino as evidence of the renaissance of this area. Exhibits are dedicated to the rich history of the city, credited to the African Americans who played a crucial role in its growth since the late 1800s.

Duncan McClellan Glass is a gallery showcasing works in glass, jewelry, and photography.

Among my favorite museums where you can learn and reflect is the Armed Forces History Museum in Largo. My Dad and nephew served in the U.S. Marine Corps, but never talked about the experience much. It is fascinating to see the roles each of the Armed Forces have played in defending our country's freedom. The experience makes me cry, but I keep going back.

The award winning Studio@620 is another venue for visual and performing arts, open to member artists, audiences and volunteers contributing to the cultural growth of the community. Visit the website to see a variety of upcoming events that include independent film screenings, musical performances, art displays and readings.

Clearwater Marine Aquarium – home of Winter, the Dolphin

Here's a feel-good story about someone who moved here, found wonderful medical care, had a new home built, and meets lots of new friends every day. Winter is a dolphin rescued by a fisherman who found her tangled in fishing wire and unable to swim. Her story is captured in *Dolphin Tale* and its sequel, 3-D major motion pictures starring Morgan Freeman, Harry Connick, Jr., and Ashley Judd, filmed here at the Clearwater Marine Aquarium. The filming process transformed a tiny marine animal rescue center to a major attraction. You can still go behind the scenes and see this working animal hospital and learn more about its mission to rescue, rehabilitate, and release injured marine life. And you can meet Winter to see how well she has adapted to life in St. Petersburg.

Clearwater Marine Aquarium

An African American Heritage Project is underway that will provide a walking tour of historic sites still standing or commemorating those lost since the first African Americans arrived in St. Pete in 1868 to build the railroads that brought the first tourists and eventual residents to the city. Touring areas known as the "Deuces" along the 22nd Street South corridor and 9th Avenue South, you will see local entertainment facilities like the Manhattan Casino and the Royal Theater, which brought in nationally accredited jazz and Gospel musicians including Louis Armstrong, Count Basie, James Brown, Ray Charles, Duke Ellington and Ella Fitzgerald. A second tour through the heart of the religious community takes you to nine historic African American churches and the renovated Jordan Elementary. The historic landmark built in 1925 is the oldest remaining school in the region, headquarters for the Pinellas County Head Start program.

Heritage Village is a living history museum with characters performing in period costume to communicate the feel of what it must have been like to live here back in the 19th Century. Imagine no air conditioning, no mosquito control! Enjoy the collection of labor saving devices used by housewives back then.

Festivals and Special Events

Sunshine year round gives festival planners the confidence to plan lots of fun events and St. Pete residents come out in large numbers to play at such parties as:

EATSt.Pete, the Enjoy Arts & Tastes Festival, celebrating food, wine and the arts in St. Petersburg and the bay area.

Firestone Grand Prix of St. Petersburg when downtown streets become a raceway and speeding is legal!

Green Thumb Festival celebrating Arbor Day and Earth Day in Walter Fuller Park, a Pinellas County park that routinely hosts quality family events like dog shows, nature walks, high school cross country meets and community picnics.

Clearwater Jazz Holiday, a major international jazz festival and draw for tens of thousands of visitors.

Sanding Ovations Sand Sculpting Contest on Treasure Island's unbelievably wide sandy beach.

John's Pass Seafood Festival, for over a quarter-century, has offered festivities for the whole family at this annual festival dedicated to fishermen lost at sea.

Bands on the Sand, a music-filled day on Treasure Island.

New on the horizon is the BLUE Ocean Film Festival, a global showcase for environmental documentaries that chose St. Petersburg as its home, moving from California.

City of Treasure Island

Sports Teams

How About Those Rays?

St. Petersburg is a baseball town with the Tampa Bay Rays as the hometown team playing at what was originally named the Florida Suncoast Dome, then the ThunderDome and now called Tropicana Field. People moving here from cities with outdoor stadiums appreciate the air-conditioned seating and ease of parking to get to the ball game on time. Major League Baseball's roots in Tampa Bay can

67

be traced back to 1913 when the Chicago Cubs moved their Spring Training operation from New Orleans to Tampa. The following year the St. Louis Browns came to St. Petersburg for spring workouts.

St. Petersburg has hosted at least one team for Spring Training in 78 of the past 84 years and had two teams train for 63 years. The city has been home to minor league baseball for 60 of the past 78 years beginning with the St. Petersburg Saints in the Florida State League in 1920. Tampa has been a Major League Spring Training site for 72 of the past 85 years and has had minor league baseball for 55 of the past 79 years.

Today, the New York Yankees play in Tampa, the Philadelphia Phillies train in Clearwater and the Toronto Blue Jays are in Dunedin, just north of St. Pete. South, you will find the Pittsburgh Pirates in Bradenton and the Baltimore Orioles in Sarasota, all beginning in mid-February. What better time of the year to fly down and check-out the real estate opportunities while taking in a couple of Grapefruit League ball games of your favorite teams?

The City's quest for a Major League Baseball franchise was finally achieved when the Tampa Bay Rays (formerly the Devil Rays) moved into Tropicana Field in 1998. Spring Training for the Rays takes place in Charlotte County, a little more than 100 miles south, also on the West Coast of Florida. The Rays have had some great seasons, earning a pennant in the American League Championship Series against the Boston Red Sox in 2008 and qualifying for post season baseball in 2010, 2011, and 2013.

On your checklist of things to do when you arrive in St. Petersburg, add:

√ Become a Tampa Bay Rays Season Ticket Holder, for a fun family experience or a terrific corporate incentive. Kids love to arrive early to catch practice balls in the stands. My Mom, who is a huge Ray's fan, caught one and she keeps it on the nightstand next to her Coach Joe Maddon gnome. Remember to visit the onsite aquarium at Tropicana Field to pet a live stingray. Don't miss taking your baseball fans to see the historic collection of autographed baseballs in Schrader's Little Cooperstown exhibit at the St. Petersburg Museum of History.

We have plenty of other professional sports here. The region is home to the NFL's Tampa Bay Buccaneers football team, NHL's Tampa Bay Lightning hockey team, Arena Football's Tampa Bay Storm and NASL's Rowdies soccer team who play at Al Lang Stadium in downtown St. Petersburg.

Collegiate sports schedules are offered by both the University of South Florida (USF) and the University of Tampa (UT).

Two post-season college football bowl games call Tampa Bay home. The Beef 'O' Brady's Bowl is held late December at Tropicana Field in downtown St. Petersburg and features a bowl-eligible team from the Big East Conference competing with one from Conference USA.

The Outback Bowl is played in Raymond James Stadium on New Year's Day and pits teams from the SEC and Big Ten Conference. Ray Jay, as it is commonly referred to, is also the home field for the Buccaneers and the NCAA USF Bulls. Two Super Bowls have been hosted by Ray Jay, in 2001 and 2009. But the first two Super Bowls held in Tampa were in 1984 and 1991 and were played at Ray Jay's predecessor, the former Tampa Stadium/Houlihan's Stadium/Big Sombrero.

In addition a year-round calendar of amateur, youth and premier sports competitions are held here. Ranging from Dragon Boat racing events to NCAA Final Four basketball games, these special events bring athletes from around the world to the area.

For information about upcoming athletic events, the Tampa Bay Sports Commission provides news about international wakeboard competitions to NCAA championships being held in the Tampa Bay area.

Restaurants

Outdoor cafes and waterfront restaurants are everywhere in St. Petersburg and new culinary experiences open every season. Check the Tampa Bay Times restaurant reviews for the latest news about the latest ethnic restaurants, organic food options, steakhouses, sandwich shops and other cuisine. Standouts include:

Caddy's on the Beach for people watching as well as great food

Bella Brava

Bob Heilman's Beachcomber

Cassis American Brasserie

Chaing Mai Thai Restaurant

Chattaway Drive-In, serving St. Pete for over 90 years

Columbia Restaurant

El Cap, described as "Cool local dive. Cash only, but definitely "St. Pete"

Ferg's, the place to be if you're a Rays fan

Foxy's Café on Treasure Island

Frenchy's on Clearwater Beach

Gigi's Pizza, on Treasure Island since 1967 and other locations on 4th Street North and St. Pete Beach

Guy Harvey Outpost at the TradeWinds Island Resort on St. Pete Beach

Marchand's inside The Vinoy Resort

Marlin Darlin Key West Grill

Mazzaro's Italian Market is small, popular and has limited hours, but worth trying to get a seat or take out.

Parkshore Grill with outdoor dining

Red Mesa Cantina with one downtown and another location in Northeast St. Pete

Rococo Steak

Salt Rock Grill

Sloppy Joes in The Bilmar Hotel on Treasure Island

Sylvia's soul food

Ted Peter's Famous Smoked Fish

The Birchwood

The Hangar Restaurant and Flight Lounge, actually *overlooking a runway at* Albert Whitted Airport

The Moon Underwater

Frenchy's

71

Fido-friendly restaurants include 400 Beach Seafood and Tap House, Acropolis, Bella Brava, Craftsman House, Dooners, Fresco's Waterfront, Kahwa Café and Espresso Bar, Meze 1991, Moscato's Bella Cucina, Parkshore Grill, and St. Pete Brasserie. Cassis American Brasserie actually has a dedicated dog menu. For more information, consult *The New Barker*, a magazine devoted to helping you cavort with your canine.

Anna Cooke

Outdoors and Fitness

One of the first things that happens when you move to Florida is you lose weight. No kidding! If you're disciplined enough to avoid umbrella drinks, that is. You're no longer a tourist after all, so it's time to figure out how to take advantage of this gorgeous weather and get some exercise. Walking and running through scenic neighborhoods with sidewalks and paths around residential lakes, numerous parks, golf course communities or Pinellas County's official trail. The Fred Marquis Pinellas Trail is a linear park and recreation trail currently extending from St. Petersburg to Tarpon Springs and is a multi-use trail everyone can enjoy, no matter what your mode of non-motorized transportation. St. Pete has a very organized Road Runner's Club or you can go it alone and see 21 pages of routes recommended for runners at WalkJogRun.net. My husband Mike, key researcher for this book, pointed out Running for Brews St. Pete, a social running club that combines running, drinking, networking, and giving. They run 5K and end up at a bar. Gotta love how they contribute to the local economy. For your upper body strengthening, the World's Largest Shuffleboard Club is located here and is nearly a century old—the club, not the players. There is some serious competition happening there, which is fun to watch and a great place for families to play.

If you prefer indoor gyms and group fitness classes, there is a handy list of nearly 200 facilities from AMA Fitness Center to Zone Pilates at Pinellas County Florida Fitness Centers and Gyms. Add walks on the beach, gardening, golf and tennis, swimming and watersports, it's no wonder we all stay so slim and trim here in St. Petersburg!

Visit St. Pete Clearwater

Golf

Among the biggest draws for people moving to Florida is the availability of golf every month of the year and St. Petersburg does not disappoint. My husband, who is from southern California, still marvels that he can pick up the phone and book a tee time a couple of days out. He recalls waiting in line at dawn in LA to get a tee time for the following weekend! Find a collection of beautiful public golf courses in Pinellas County at this website. www.tampabay.com/golf/courses/pinellas/

A sampling of some scenic and historic courses include:

Belleview Biltmore Golf Club is located at the historic resort, built by railroad tycoon Henry Plant in 1897 and listed on the National Register of Historic Places.

The Belleview Biltmore and Dunedin Country Club were both designed by the prolific and talented course architect Donald Ross. Dunedin can claim being home of the PGA of America from 1945 to 1962.

The Par 71 East Bay Golf Club in Largo is one of the most popular public layouts and Lansbrook Golf Club in Palm Harbor was named one of the Best Places to Play by Golf Digest Magazine. In Seminole, The Tides Golf Club offers views of Boca Ciega Bay and the Gulf of Mexico and Seminole Lake Country Club challenges players of every age and skill level in settings that remind you of "old Florida."

On the north end of town, Mangrove Bay Golf Course is an award winning regulation 18-hole championship golf facility, with one of the finest practice ranges in the area, complete with practice putting and chipping greens. Invest in a Big Summer Golf Card for savings and unlimited play during the months of May through October.

Private country clubs allow reciprocal play certain months of the year, usually in the summer. Or consider joining one of several spectacular private clubs in St. Petersburg like Feather Sound Country Club, The Bayou Club, Cove Cay Club, or Isla Del Sol Yacht and Country Club and Pasadena Yacht and Country Club, which offer the private club experience for boaters, as well as golfers.

The Vinoy Renaissance Resort & Golf Club, featured on the cover of this book, originally opened on New Year's Eve in 1925 and is the only historic luxury hotel on Florida's West Coast that boasts a private marina, 18-hole golf course and a 12-court tennis complex. Reflecting elegant 1920s Mediterranean Revival architecture, the resort décor is elegant, yet always comfortable, with a "no jacket required" philosophy. I told you guys you would love it here!

Golf instruction for children is usually available to members of the private clubs and professional golfer Juan "Chi Chi" Rodriguez co-founded the Chi Chi Rodriguez Academy, Youth Foundation and Golf Club in Clearwater. Golfing at private clubs like St. Petersburg Country Club and The Vinoy require membership contingent on endorsement from a couple of existing members so you have to know someone. Start socializing as soon as you arrive in town. That's a popular way to enjoy a champagne lifestyle on beer money...friends with boats or country club memberships!

Par 3 executive courses include Twin Brooks a municipal golf course at Treasure Bay Golf and Tennis, a public club on Treasure Island and Cypress Links, located in the Mangrove Bay Golf Course complex on 62nd Ave. North.

If you're golf challenged, there's always Smuggler's Cove Adventure Golf on Madeira Beach and Polynesian Putter on St. Pete Beach. Fun!

Tennis

Most of the tennis court facilities you see throughout St. Petersburg are open to the public, belonging to local schools or churches or at the various St. Petersburg parks. The city manages 66 tennis courts at 15 sites, all open from sunrise until 11 p.m. Tennis is a popular sport here. So, if getting a court time is still a challenge, join one of the local tennis clubs and participate in their tournament and open play schedules. It is also a great way to make new friends. Anyone can join St. Petersburg Tennis Center which was established in 1928 and is the oldest continuously run clubs in the city. Play on one of 14 Har-Tru courts for a fee or on the four hard surface courts for free. Tennis legend Chris Evert played here as a teenager so center court is named after her. Treasure Bay Club on Treasure Island is also open for public play on ten courts for a small fee, but all are lit for night play, which is prime time during the warmer months.

Parks

If you are not convinced that St. Petersburg is environmentally friendly yet, check out the bicycle and pedestrian-only streets in Fort De Soto Park, or the ever-expanding Fred Marquis Trails www. pinellascounty.org/trailgd/ that will eventually cover a 75-mile loop from south St. Petersburg to Tarpon Springs. The trail is for walkers, bicyclists, skaters, riders of wheelchairs and non-motorized vehicles of all types. Currently extending from St. Petersburg to Tarpon Springs, The Trail, created along an abandoned railroad corridor, provides a unique, protected green space maintained by Pinellas County Parks & Conservation Resources.

Pinellas County Communications

Lake Tarpon is the largest lake in Pinellas County with a surface area of four square miles. Its watershed encompasses 52 square miles, including its two largest tributaries, South Creek and Brooker Creek. The lake is a valuable recreational destination and is renowned for its largemouth bass fishing. You may need a freshwater license, so be sure to inquire with the tax collector's office. Florida residents over age 65 do not need a fishing license, but must show proof of age and residency if requested.

Pinellas County Communications

76

Learn more about events happening at all of the Pinellas County Parks by checking www.pinellascounty.org/events.

The numerous parks throughout the city encompass 17 recreation centers, 9 swimming pools, and 70 athletic fields, according to St. Petersburg Parks and Recreation. Located on the north shore of Lake Maggiore, Dell Holmes Park is the home of St. Petersburg's first zero-depth water playground. A list of the dog-friendly parks can be found on the website, too. You can take Spot for a walk on the beach at Ft. De Soto, along Gandy Bridge Causeway, and in Pinellas Park, Seminole and Largo. Many outdoor eateries downtown welcome your best friend, as does the Saturday Morning Farmer's Market.

Fresh Air: Exploring, hiking, kayaking, fishing, boating

David R. Schrichte

Catching a glimpse of Florida wildlife is exhilarating and it can happen anytime, anywhere. Wild monkeys, burrowing owls, otters, foxes, an array of tropical birds and, yes, alligators and snakes, too, make this area their home. They were here first, after all.

Northeast St. Petersburg residents have frequent visits from a large flock of wild parakeets, rumored to have escaped a Miami aviary after a tropical storm. You may miss them as they zigzag from tree to tree, but you are sure to hear the chattering, so keep eyes and ears open. Manatees and otters show up in Coffee Pot Bayou if you are lucky enough to spot them.

David R. Schrichte

You can seek out a rewarding experience communing with manatees at such non-touristy sites as Tampa Electric Company's Power Plant near Apollo Beach, about 40 miles from St. Petersburg. According to members of a very active and devoted Save the Manatee Club, when the water temperature gets cool in Tampa Bay, manatees gather in the warm falling waters of the plant's discharge pipes.

This natural phenomenon is so prevalent, researchers from the Florida Fish and Wildlife Research Institute in St. Petersburg come here to observe, photograph and update population figures for this protected species. Kari Rood, who heads up the Manatee Photo-Identification program at the FWC's Fish and Wildlife Florida, says the minimum counts of manatees at the plant have ranged anywhere from a low of 33 in November to 258 manatees on a chilly mid-December day.

Hiking, walking along the shore, peering from a pier, paddle boarding or kayaking are the easiest and least expensive ways to observe nature on the waterfront.

Because Pinellas County has an amazing 47 launch sites for kayaks and canoes, there's bound to be one near you. So, you can take your water adventure on the Pinellas County Blueways. The website www.pinellascounty. org/Plan/pdf_files/blueways_ map.pdf can be printed and taken with you on your travels to let you know what facilities are available at each launch site, such as restrooms, picnic

Pinellas County Communications

tables, grills, camping facilities, showers, restaurants and overnight accommodations.

Get a different perspective from under the water by scuba diving. Scuba Cat Charters will take a maximum six people on specialized dive experiences to various reefs and underwater rock fields teeming with tropical fish, sponges and coral, and interesting offshore wrecks like Gunsmoke, seized and sunk by authorities for smuggling marijuana in 1977.

Pinellas County Communications

The best way to explore coastal islands, like Weedon Island, nearly 3,200 acres of preserved marine ecosystem located on Tampa Bay, is via kayak. Kayak rental shops like Sweetwater Kayaks on Gandy Boulevard in Northeast St. Petersburg are abundant on the beaches and Coquina Key, too. Or buy your own kayak and more at Bill Jackson's Shop for Adventure, family owned and operated for people with a passion for the outdoors since 1951. Another iconic spot to discover is Suncoast Surf Shop on Treasure Island, one of the oldest and longest running surf shops in Florida. Get your stand up paddleboards here. Rent one here first, head for the Gulf, decide that you love it, and buy one.

Boating

Visit St. Pete Clearwater

Both freshwater and saltwater options are available with more than a dozen large lakes for boating. You can rent boats at I.C. Sharks (clever referral from neighbors, the Cleary's) or by joining a club at Mariner's Cove in Gulfport. If buying a boat is first on your list when moving to a city with water, water everywhere, head to O'Neill's Marina that's been around for more than 50 years or Thunder Marine, another family owned business, keeping people afloat for four decades. Visit Quality Marina in Clearwater or Central Marine Services on Tyrone

80

Boulevard in St. Petersburg, new and used boat dealers for Yamaha outboards, Parker,Shipoke, Sundance boats, Cobia, World Cat, Carolina Cat, Livingston, Skeeter, Premier Pontoons and Glacier Bay boats.

Pinellas County lists 20 public access boat ramps that will lead to quiet backwater fishing excursions, deep sea diving, lakes for water skiing, island hopping, or power boat racing. Take advantage of bayside boating near downtown's Vinoy Park, drop anchor, and enjoy music from outdoor concerts. The largest boat ramp can be found in Fort De Soto Park, where boaters can toodle around five interconnected keys, camp overnight, and learn the history of the conquistadors who first explored these barrier islands in the early 16th Century.

Kelly Franckowiak

Further offshore is Passage Key National Wildlife Refuge, part of the United States National Wildlife Refuge System, one of the first of its kind established in 1905. Because of its small size and importance to wildlife, the refuge is closed to all public use. But you *can* steer your boat to Caladesi Island State Park where you can enjoy swimming, sunbathing and beachcombing. Saltwater anglers can cast a line from their boats or surf fish. Onshore you will find picnic tables and pavilions can be reserved for a fee.

Visit St. Pete Clearwater

If you are relocating with your own boat, you will find many marinas and space for dry dock storage.

Marina	Location
City of St. Petersburg Marina, Store, and Dock	Downtown Waterfront
Hubbards Marina's Pass in Madeira Beach	170 John's Pass Boardwalk
Harborage Marina	1110 3rd Street South
Blind Pass Marina Enterprises	St. Pete Beach
Maximo Marina Ventures LLC	4801 37th Street South
Pasadena Marina Inc	South Pasadena
O'Neill's Marina	Sunshine Skyway
Mariner's Cove Marina	Gulfport
Tierra Verde Marina	South, near Fort DeSoto Park
Loggerhead® Marina	Frenchman's Creek
Snell Isle Marina	Northeast St. Petersburg

Housed in a lovely downtown waterfront location, St. Petersburg Yacht Club is one of the oldest and most established members-only yacht clubs in the country. Two existing members must endorse newcomers. It oversees additional marinas and dock locations on Snell Isle and in Pass-a-Grille Beach. Founded in 1909, this traditional club has served generations of family boaters, with a lively activity calendar and opportunities to socialize and make new friends. Depending on where you settle, you may find other clubs more convenient, including Isla del Sol Yacht and Country Club on the southern tip of St. Petersburg for yachting, fishing and golf enthusiasts or Pasadena Yacht & Country Club, centrally located between the beaches and downtown. You can pursue your golf game here, too.

Perhaps the yachting lifestyle is still in your future. Learn to sail at St. Pete Yacht Club or Simple Sailing Charters, LLC

Pinellas County Communications

Here is something you can brag about to your friends up north—year round you can launch your boat from the Park Boulevard ramp, pull up to several dock friendly restaurants and enjoy easy access to John's Pass Village located between Treasure Island and Madeira Beach or venture further north to Clearwater restaurants. Some places will even let you catch your own fish and they'll cook it for you.

Tim Marusarz

Fishing Charters and Sunset Cruises

Find the best places to cast your line by going to the St. Petersburg/ Clearwater Area Convention and Visitors Bureau. This resource highlights the fishing opportunities on almost 600 miles of coastline. Fish near shore, offshore or from piers.

Truly adventurous charter boats go shark fishing near the Sunshine Skywaybridge and off of John's Pass. Hubbard's Marina, found in John's Pass offers every kind of water-loving adventure. Several experienced boat captains like those found at Boca Sportfishing take individuals and groups on deep sea fishing excursions guaranteed to find good eating fish like grouper, snapper, barracuda, king mackerel, and tuna, that they will fillet and package for take home.

Tim Marusarz

Florida residents over age 65 do not need a fishing license, but must show proof of age and residency if requested. Whatever your pursuit on St. Petersburg's waterways, be sure to stop by Bill Jackson's for fishing, camping and diving gear, life preservers, and skis, as well as classroom instruction about how to enjoy water sports safely. Please take the time to attend a U.S. Coast Guard Auxiliary boating safety class to learn the rules of navigation and how to read nautical charts and tides. St. Petersburg's bay areas have plenty of sandbars and disappearing islands you won't want to discover accidentally.

If you prefer to leave the boating to the experts, simply hop on board one of several vessels operated by Suncoast Adventure Center, Dolphin Landings, or Starlight Cruises for a scenic tour of the waterfront out of nearby Clearwater Beach. Thrill seekers will appreciate the speedy ride of a 72-foot speedboat, touted to be the world's largest, the Sea Screamer, also in Clearwater. Or practice your best "Aaaargh!" and ship ahoy aboard Captain Memo's Original Pirate Cruise.

Tim Marusarz

Local Attractions

Enjoy free admission to Pinellas County's Florida Botanical Gardens where you can learn about the indigenous plants and flowers that make this City so beautiful. This unique local treasure has over 30 acres of cultivated gardens and 90 acres of natural areas to explore. Kid-friendly markers identified by an animated "Flora" lead children from a butterfly garden through fruit and flower gardens.

Sunken Gardens is St. Petersburg's oldest living museum with more than 50,000 well-established plants flourishing on four acres for more than a century. It is located adjacent to Great Explorations, the children's museum, offering a perfect way to spend the day.

Historic Walking Tours organized by St. Petersburg Preservation, Inc. are scheduled every Saturday, providing educational glimpses of the City's rich history. The group also screens classic movies in Straub Park on Thursday evenings in October and in May.

Birding

The 2,000 mile <u>Great Florida Birding and Wildlife Trail</u> runs through St. Pete/Clearwater, one of 489 sites along the trail identified as places to see tropical birds, rare and exotic species in the State of Florida. According to the website link, because I have not gone birding yet myself, you can spot hundreds of birds in their natural Florida habitats including mangrove swamps, slash-pine forests, the beaches and the Tampa Bay estuary. Great Blue Herons, Pelicans, Snowy Egrets, and Pileated Woodpeckers live here year round and are easily spotted. Keep your eyes open and you can experience the joy of seeing the rare Roseate Spoonbill, Bald Eagle, Great Horned Owl, Peregrine Falcon or other raptors. In fact, St. Petersburg holds a <u>Raptor Fest</u> celebrating birds of prey at Boyd Hill Nature Preserve every year in February.

<u>St. Petersburg Audubon Society</u> leads tours and educational classes about seasonal shorebirds and other migratory species that fall under the true category of snowbirds visiting only during the winter months. The Annual Audubon St. Petersburg Christmas Bird Count is the

second longest running count in the State of Florida. For more than 75 years, citizen science groups visit several of the predetermined sites where birds can be seen and record the species and their numbers. In three of the past four years, St. Petersburg has tied or exceeded the organization's high species count. Sign up to join the count in St. Petersburg.

Speaking of birds, you can fly over St. Petersburg and get a birds-eye view of this coastal city in one of several helicopters or small planes taking off and landing at Albert Whitted Airport. Safari Choppers and Florida Biplanes provide hourly rides or private charters for longer tours of specific areas. It's fun to watch them take off and land while enjoying a meal at the Hangar Restaurant and Flight Lounge located at the airport. If you have a sensitive stomach like mine, you'll plan to eat *after* the flight.

CHAPTER 7

SCHOOLS AND FACTS FOR FAMILIES

Once you've chosen the home of your dreams in St. Petersburg, finding quality education for your children will not be a challenge. Florida law specifies that all children who have attained the age of six years or who will have attained the age of six years by February 1 of any school year are required to attend school regularly during the entire school term. First grade enrollment is limited to students who turn six on or before September 1 and who have completed kindergarten.

Infant & Toddler Care

Half a dozen Head Start programs are maintained throughout St. Petersburg, promoting school readiness for children ages birth to 5 from low-income families. One of these centers, R'Club Child Care, Inc. was established in 1976 in Pinellas County as a not-for-profit organization to provide high quality, accessible and affordable school age child care. R'Club has expanded to include locations outside of Pinellas County and provides full day preschool and before and after school and extended learning programs for 3,000 children daily at more than 40 centers, serving children ages 2 - 14 (infants and 1 year olds served in selected centers), and exceptional students ages 3 - 22.

Be diligent in researching day care centers and don't be shy about asking neighbors, friends and co-workers for recommendations. The good news is that you will have nearly 400 facilities available to your family. A good place to start is Coordinated Child Care of Pinellas,

Inc., a private not-for-profit that started in 1969 as "Project Playpen, Inc." It is recognized as the leading agency in the development of quality early childhood and school age programs to prepare children for school.

Public and Private Schools

Academic accountability is paramount to the educators in our community. Sixty-five percent of Pinellas County's graded public schools received an A or B in the Florida A+ Plan. The district's average SAT combined critical reading, mathematics and writing score was 1517 and continues to be above state and national averages. For more information, see www.pcsb.org

You will want to learn about The Florida Comprehensive Assessment Test (FCAT), part of Florida's effort to improve the teaching and learning of higher educational standards. The primary purpose of the FCAT is to assess student achievement of the high-order cognitive skills represented in the Sunshine State Standards (SSS) in Reading, Writing, Mathematics, and Science.

Pinellas County Schools is the city's largest employer with more than 8,000 teachers and another 5,300 supporting staff members teaching children in 140 schools. Even more educators can be found in numerous private schools. In fact, in the 2011-2012 school year, 15,236 students attended the 112 available private and special education schools in the greater St. Petersburg area. For a comprehensive list, visit Florida School Choice and enter Pinellas under the district designation.

Because of waiting lists, parents must participate in a lottery selection to have their children attend Fundamental schools. Once a child is chosen for the fundamental path, siblings are given preference, based on space available. A fundamental program is a family-oriented school with a structured environment and joint parent-teacher-student commitment. Fundamental schools focus on student self-responsibility and discipline, daily homework, a dress code which exceeds that of the school district and required attendance at conferences and monthly parent meetings. Note that parents must provide transportation for their children to the six countywide elementary and three middle school fundamental schools, with some exceptions. Here is a list of the fundamental schools in Pinellas County:

Elementary Schools

- Bay Vista
- Curtis
- Lakeview
- Madeira Beach
- Pasadena
- Tarpon Springs

Middle Schools

- Clearwater
- Madeira Beach
- Thurgood Marshall

High Schools

- St. Petersburg High School
- Boca Ciega
- Dunedin
- Osceola

While St. Petersburg's public schools have large enrollment, the average class size is only 22 students. The academic year 2011-2012 taught a total of 103,776 students according to the Annie E. Casey Foundation. In kindergarten to 3rd grade the ratio of teacher to students is even less at 1:18. High school classrooms average 25 students per teacher.

The total operating budget for the 2011-2012 school year was more than a billion dollars at $1,331,798,780 yielding an average planned expenditure per student within a single school year of $7,625.

Demographics of students in Pinellas County Public Schools:

- 58.7% white
- 18.9% black

91

- 13.9% Hispanic
- 4.3% Asian
- 3.8% multi-racial
- 0.3% Native American

For an overview of the schools in St. Petersburg, review the school district map or use the Zoned Student Locator based on your home address. No school assignment or reservation is either expressed or implied on this site. It is a tool to lookup what school zones your address falls within. Students must be registered by mid-July to attend the coming school year. Other important information for parents who are new to the district can be found at the Pinellas County Schools Newsroom.

Private Schools

A good source for the private schools in the area can be found on the Florida School Choice website. (www.floridaschoolchoice.org/Information/PrivateSchoolDirectory)

Enter Pinellas as the county to pull up a list of all private schools. You can also find a fairly comprehensive rating list of more than 130 private schools in the area at this website, www.greatschools.org/florida/st.-petersburg/schools/?st=private which also provides listings of homes for sale in the area. See the lists below with some examples of annual tuition. Catholic schools in St. Petersburg are most numerous among the private school opportunities, most attached to the parishes of Roman Catholic Churches. Some examples are provided below along with tuition, based on one student and will vary when adding siblings:

- Blessed Sacrament Catholic School – Kindergarten to 8th grade tuition is $5,445
- St. Jude Cathedral School
- St. John Vianney Catholic School – 1st to 8th grade tuition is $4,300
- Transfiguration Catholic School

- St. John Catholic School
- St. Raphael Catholic School – K to 8th in parish tuition is $5,350 per year; out of parish is $7,050.
- St. Petersburg Catholic High School – In parish tuition is $9,800 per year; out of parish is $12,700.
- St. Paul Catholic School
- Holy Family Catholic School
- Most Holy Name of Jesus Catholic School

There are also a number of non-denominational and Christian schools in the region, such as Northside Christian School serving grades K -12 with annual tuitions that vary by grade, starting at $8,550 up to $11,625. Pre-K to 8th grade education can be had at Lutheran private schools that include Grace Lutheran School, with middle school tuition starting at around $7,200 for example, or at Lutheran Church of the Cross Day School ($8,975 for middle school age students) and Our Savior Lutheran School ($6,800 or less if paid in advance.) Again, check the website for details as the prices for tuition change, sometimes by semester.

Award-winning prep schools are Canterbury School of Florida and Shorecrest Preparatory School, both found on the Northeast side of the city, accepting students at Kindergarten through 12th grade. Brighton Preparatory School is located in the center of St. Petersburg, serving grades 1-8 while Academy Prep Center of St. Petersburg on the south side of the city is for 5th to 8th grade students only. Academy Prep relies on donations. Students attend on full scholarships generated by private funds raised each year from the local community to provide scholarships of $16,000 per student.

Admiral Farragut Academy, also located on a waterfront, is a school for day students or boarders, starting from Pre-K up to 12th grade. Boarding school starts at the 7th and 8th grade levels and has an annual tuition of $42,160. The academy earns accolades for its participation in division sports and ROTC programs.

College/Post High School

Eckerd College

I admit I am predisposed to recommend Eckerd College where a number of very talented professors afforded me a wonderful liberal arts education and my alma mater, University of South Florida, which has campuses in St. Petersburg, Sarasota, and Tampa. Probably most important to students choosing colleges now is the ability to find jobs when they graduate and Eckerd College has statistics:

- 33% of recent graduates found jobs within one month of graduation.
- 69% of recent graduates are employed full time
- 36% went on to graduate school

Eckerd College graduates have gone on to become famous authors like Dennis Lehane, *New York Times* bestselling author of *Mystic River, Shutter Island,* and *Gone, Baby, Gone.* Many graduates are teachers, lawyers, and physicians or have been welcomed by graduate study programs worldwide. Go here (www.eckerd.edu/pel/academics) for a list of the academic degrees available from Eckerd College.

Eckerd also offers a program for experienced learners designed to fit the lifestyles of adult learners who want to earn an Eckerd College bachelor's degree while continuing to work.

University of South Florida

It may seem a distraction to look out a classroom window and see people sailing, swimming, canoeing, kayaking and paddle-boarding, but plenty of serious learning happens at the University of South Florida St. Petersburg campus. Perched on the waterfront and minutes away from the cultural offerings downtown, the college serves undergraduate and graduate level education. It has all the advantages of the large public university in Tampa, including nationally ranked NCAA football, men's basketball, women's softball and women's sailing. Some serious study takes place here, too. Check out the website (www.usfsp.edu/academic-programs) for the latest list of Bachelor's and Master's programs.

USF St. Petersburg

St. Petersburg College

Also preparing students to land the perfect job and pursue the right career is St. Petersburg College with students graduating annually with AA degrees. Many students work while studying and appreciate having the convenience of 10 locations for study throughout Pinellas County. Tuition costs about 40 percent less than Florida's universities. It offers more than 100 academic programs, from career training to university transfer options to bachelor's degrees in more than a dozen fields. See the full list here (www.spcollege.edu/academics).

Stetson University College of Law

The prestigious Stetson University College of Law is located in Gulfport, a community in Greater St. Petersburg. Founded in 1900 as Florida's first law school, Stetson is fully accredited by the American Bar Association and is ranked No. 1 for trial advocacy and No. 5 for legal writing by *U.S. News & World Report.*

Student Housing

Students living on campus at Eckerd College will love the waterfront location and lots of green space to find a place to escape and study. Wise professors hold classes outdoors when the weather permits to take advantage of the lovely environment. Accommodations range from traditional shared rooms to apartments with incredible views of Boca Ciega Bay.

Laura Osteen

At USF, an 81,000 square-foot University Student Center opened in the last couple of years, with a ballroom, dining facilities, meeting rooms, outdoor verandas and a six-story residence hall. The residence hall accommodates nearly 200 residents in two-person bedrooms.

Stetson owns several homes and apartments within walking distance of the law school. Students are encouraged to add their names to a waiting list as housing is available on a first come, first served basis.

While St. Pete College is a commuter school, they have identified several helpful individuals known as Student Life and Leadership Coordinators who will assist you in finding apartments or rental homes, as well as other problem solving so you can concentrate on your studies. See the list of contacts at each of the eight college campus locations throughout St. Petersburg at their website (www.spcollege.edu/pages/studentlife.aspx?id=913).

Adult Education—Non-degree programs

College is not for everyone and some terrific career opportunities can be discovered with some specific job training from Pinellas Technical Education Centers (PTEC). My brother Ed went this route, obtaining excellent culinary training that opened doors for him at many fine restaurants, resort hotels, and clubs. I am proud to see him happy in his job as an executive chef for a private club catering soirées, winning awards, and appearing in local media. It was called Pinellas Vocational Technical Institute back then and only had one location in Clearwater. Today, PTEC offers full time programs, apprenticeships, and short courses for young students and adult education at campuses in St. Petersburg, Clearwater, Tarpon Springs or online. Visit the website at www.myptec.org/programs_and_courses for a complete list of study and practical training that will prepare you to work in many different industries.

Adult learners will be pleased to know that the Pinellas County School system has six education centers that cater to their needs. General Educational Development (GED) test preparation includes reading, science, social studies, math and language. For students who cannot attend traditional classes, Pinellas County Schools also offers online GED classes that students can take from home. Visit www.floridastudyonline.com for more information. English for Speakers of Other Languages (ESOL) is a program to help adults speak, write and read English. Courses are offered at any of the centers below or online, as well, at the same website.

Some of us simply want to keep going to school all our lives to discover new interests or hobbies or to find things to talk about and not necessarily to prepare us for careers. Students over the age of 50 make up a large part of the audience in lecture halls and auditoriums throughout St. Petersburg, so don't stay away fearing you'll be the oldest kid in the class. Here is a list of the County-managed adult education centers:

Clearwater Adult Education Center
727-469-4190

Dixie Hollins Adult Education Center
727-547-7872

Lakewood Community School
727-893-2955

Northeast Community School
727-570-3193

Palm Harbor Community School
727-669-1140

Tomlinson Adult Learning Center
727-893-2723

Lifelong learning programs are available at the St. Petersburg College and USF campuses, too. USF waives tuition for students age 60 or older. Eckerd College is one of only 115 Osher Lifelong Learning Institutes found on the most innovative colleges and universities across the U.S. According to their website, the programs at Eckerd promise:

- An intellectually stimulating learning environment that will enrich your life

- Classes, trips, workshops, speaker series, special events, social activities and more - and no tests or grades!

- Opportunities to volunteer/do pro bono work

- A friendly place to meet interesting people and develop new friendships

Fun Activities for Youngsters

Tim Marusarz

When you discover all of the opportunities for children to take swimming lessons, fish, go skim boarding, play soccer, football, and baseball, you truly realize St. Petersburg is not solely for retirees to spend their Golden Years. Notice I mention swim lessons first. When you move to a city surrounded by water with in ground swimming pools, lakes, and canals in most backyards, put swimming lessons first on your list of things to do. Check these locations to find the spot most convenient to learn to swim: Mermaid Swim School, YMCA of Greater St. Petersburg with four locations, and Tampa Bay Turners offering gymnastics lessons, too.

Pinellas County public schools offer plenty of extra-curricular athletic programs led by dedicated coaches. Check with your child's individual school regarding participation in district conferences and tournaments for boys and girls basketball and soccer, wrestling, flag football, softball, baseball, tennis, track, and volleyball. There are also regional travel ball competitions and sports leagues outside of the school programs offered by the city's and county's Parks and

Recreation departments. Jack Puryear Park is *the* place for football with five fields, lit for nighttime play.

Eleven recreation centers in Greater St. Petersburg offer supervised programs before- and after-school and every summer for youth entering first through sixth grades.

Northeast Little League also known locally as NELL has a competitive baseball and softball program attracting crowds in the bleachers against rival teams from Pinellas Park, Seminole, and Clearwater South. For more information about this and other youth leagues for basketball, cheerleading and football, soccer and even lacrosse, visit the website for St. Petersburg's Parks and Recreation Department.

Fossil Park has an impressive layout for your family's fancy footwork experts on skate boards. The Schoolyard is a 12,000 square foot indoor street style skate park and skate shop that provides lessons every Saturday. St. Pete Beach also has a skate park.

Pinellas County, in conjunction with the University of Florida Extension offers a 4-H Program of instruction in a dozen clubs throughout the county for school-age children to learn life skills and participate in county fairs.

Students ages 12 through 17 can become Junior Docents at Heritage Village in Largo, where young adults from the community volunteer their time and enjoy learning about Pinellas County and Florida history.

The Boy and Girl Scouts of America have thriving troops with terrific activities for children and their parents. A quick website search brings up at least five different troops making it convenient to join the one nearest you. Most of the troops are sponsored through the churches. Even at the Cub Scout level, the boys go camping several times a year throughout the State. Camp La-No-Che in Paisley, FL gives them an opportunity to learn archery, climbing, sailing, and kayaking.

Karen Quilty

A neighbor's son practices laps in our swimming pool as part of his youth triathlon training from USAT Certified Coach Karen Quilty, assisted by Steve Sykes, USA Cycling level two coach. Led by owner and multi-credentialed Coach Jennifer Hutchison, Triton Elite Multisport gets the kids and teens out of the house and in great shape training for triathlons – swimming, biking, and running. The team is run by USA Triathlon certified coaches who train youth and junior development athletes ranging in age from 7-19. Participants learn how to swim in pools, lakes, bays, the Gulf of Mexico and the Atlantic Ocean, preparing them for different types of competition in various bodies of water. Florida's ability to provide year round training is a big advantage yielding the best competitors in the country.

Junior golfers can tee up at The First Tee of St. Petersburg clinics held at Mangrove Bay, Cypress Links and Twin Brooks Golf Courses, again, with year round opportunities to ensure your little guy or girl makes it to the PGA Tour. Instruction from PGA professionals is a great way to introduce your child to the game of golf, starting at age six.

Parents interviewed for this book recommended VSI Pinellas Youth Soccer Club as another great way to keep kids active. The nonprofit organization provides a competitive and recreational program for players between the ages of 4 and 19. As future soccer stars begin to shine, European coaches are invited to come to the U.S. and coach the children to prepare them for professional leagues.

Believe it or not, when your little fans decide they want to pursue hockey careers after seeing the Tampa Bay Lightning play, they have places to skate on ice in Florida before they grow up and move north to become Bruins or Blackhawks. Check out Ice Sports Forum in Tampa, the Clearwater Ice Arena, or the Ellenton Ice and Sports Complex found just south of the Sunshine Skyway Bridge. These are all indoor, controlled temperature arenas because, no, you won't ever find outdoor ice rinks in St. Petersburg. Yay! That's why we move here.

For the Wee Little Ones

Every second and fourth Thursday, Brooker Creek Preserve Environmental Education Center and Weedon Island Preserve Cultural and Natural History Center share the wonders of the natural world with preschoolers. To give children that ever-important foundation of reading, find the nearest Pinellas County Library and participate in Born to Read. Funded by the Pinellas Public Library Cooperative, (PPLC) is designed to empower parents to be their child's first teacher. A dozen locations, plus several more in Clearwater's library system, offer free library cards, books and services to children, their families, and others who work with children. Note that PPLC, celebrating more than 20 years of service to the community, also operates a Deaf Literacy Center that does amazing work for more than 120,000 deaf and hard-of-hearing persons who reside in Pinellas County, Florida.

Great Explorations Children's Museum opened an 18,000 square foot facility located next to the historic Sunken Gardens on 4th Street North in St. Petersburg. Recognized as one of Florida's top museums and one of America's top museums for children, the museum gives children from preschool age to young adults as volunteers, innovative ways to learn through creativity, play and exploration.

Another thing to add to your checklist:

√A single Dad highly recommended taking the kids downtown to carve their initials in one of the Banyan Trees in Straub Park, buy some frozen yogurt or slices of pizza and enjoy a fun, family afternoon. Kids and parents are amazed by these enormous trees with their dangling roots.

A Night Off From the Kids

Loews Don Cesar Hotel

If I had kids, I would do this! In researching the book, several parents mentioned they get a hotel room at The Bilmar Beach Resort on Treasure Island, the Loews Don CeSar Hotel or TradeWinds Island Resort in St. Pete Beach once a quarter and let the kids run and have fun out on the beach while they enjoy a relaxing sunset. Just being away, if only for a night seems to give everyone in the family a refreshing break. It's also important to schedule date night without the kids, like dinner downtown or on the beaches, then meet friends for drinks and go dancing. St. Petersburg has an eclectic mix of music and theater performances you won't want to miss. Plan in advance to get tickets as concerts and events at the Tampa Bay Times Forum and Mahaffey Theater sell out quickly.

CHAPTER 8

GET INVOLVED IN THE COMMUNITY

As we said in the introduction, residents of "The Burg" are friendly and eager to serve. That feeling of warm southern hospitality is infectious. You will find it easy to meet new friends quite possibly just walking along the beach looking for shells. At work and at play, seek out your favorite activities, meeting people at school or in church, attending festivals, going to the theater and musical performances. At St. Petersburg's City Theatre auditions are open to the entire community and they claim to be a teaching stage if you can't act, dance, or sing!

Associations and Social Ties

Get out and get involved in all the activities going on around St. Petersburg by consulting local calendars such as www.stpete.org/events/ You will be welcomed at local chapters of your fraternal organization, including Rotary, Kiwanis, Optimist, Masons, Exchange Club, and Tiger Bay Club, which is a unique, non-partisan political club, founded in 1978. The GFWC St. Petersburg Woman's Club has the longest heritage of any of the women's groups in town founded with 14 chartered members in 1913 by Illinois native, Nancy A. Greene. Today, the organization numbers 150 members. There are several Tampa Bay area "Meetups," including Tampa Bay Adventures, Tampa Bay Young Professionals, and Tampa Bay Outdoor Adventures, doing such fun things as an urban restaurant tour on bicycles.

The Business and Professional Women's group has a nice mixed schedule of educational and fun events to join.

Or become a volunteer! Newcomers enjoy meeting new friends while participating in good deeds like volunteering at museums or hospitals or putting some muscle into building homes at Habitat for Humanity. Deliver cookies for Casey's Cookies, a local non-profit that promotes independence for developmentally and physically disabled adults through training and employment. To support All Children's Hospital and its efforts to treat children from all over the country, a number of Ronald McDonald Houses are located nearby for parents to stay in close proximity to their little ones. St. Petersburg residents bring food, clothing, toiletries to stock the homes and offer support services and other volunteer work to help the families. St. Petersburg Free Clinic, Brookwood House and a thrift store operated by volunteers for Casa, a shelter for abused women and children are other local charities always needing a helping hand. Look for other ways to give back to your community in the local newspaper, *Tampa Bay Times.*

Animal lovers can become superheroes by rescuing pets and offering animal care through Pinellas County Animal Services or Pet Pal Animal Shelter, a non-profit that plans memorable events like Yappy Hour, Bark Art, and the annual 5K Tap n' Run in downtown St. Pete. "In nearby Tampa, Big Cat Rescue is, paws down, one of the best advocates for lions, tigers, leopards and other varieties of exotic wild cats. Founded in 1992, Big Cat Rescue is the largest accredited sanctuary devoted to exotic cats in the world, home to over 100 cats who were abandoned, abused, orphaned, saved from being turned into fur coats, or retired from performing acts."

Area schools and churches of all denominations have volunteer opportunities or can steer you in the right direction to find something that fits your passions and skills. For more ideas, visit www. greatnonprofits.org and scroll through a list of more than 97,000 volunteer organizations in St. Petersburg.

Find friends by becoming Friends of the Library.

Big Cat Rescue

One of the best ways to get involved is to learn about the various government departments that provide services to you and your neighbors. Pinellas Citizen University unravels the mystery and takes you on a behind the scenes tour, face to face with county administrators and decision-makers. Through exciting field trips and exercises, you learn first-hand how Pinellas County provides services to nearly one million county residents.

Pinellas County Communications

Local Media

The best sources for what to do in your community are the local news outlets. Find continuous local news, traffic and weather on Bay News Channel 9. Television network affiliates are:

WFLA NBC 8
WTSP CBS 10
WTVT FOX 13
WUSF PBS 16
WFTS ABC 28
Check your cable or satellite television listings for accurate channels, based on your service.

There are approximately 60 radio stations that are within listening range of St. Petersburg. Brand new is a 24 hour online and mobile radio station focused on St. Petersburg, Florida and our beach communities called Radio St. Pete. Local news stations include:

News-Talk

WMNF 88.5 FM
WHPT 102.5 FM
WWBA 820 AM
WFLA 970 AM
WHNZ 1250 AM
WWPR 1490 AM
WRXB 1590 AM (Broadcasts a Police and Community Perspective every Tuesday at 10:00 a.m.)

Sports

WHFS 98.7 FM
WDAE 620 AM (ESPN and Tampa Bay Rays Baseball's official radio network)
WHFS 1010 AM
WHBO 1040 AM
WFUS 103.5 FM (Tampa Bay Buccaneers)

National Public Radio (NPR) is broadcast from campuses of the University of South Florida in both Tampa WUSF-FM (89.7) and Sarasota WSMR-FM (89.1).

Newspapers

Moving to St. Petersburg, you are fortunate to have one of the nation's best daily newspapers delivered to your door or electronic device. The _Tampa Bay Times_ (formerly known as the _St. Petersburg Times_) is widely considered one of the Top Ten newspapers in America and has won nine Pulitzer Prizes. It is Florida's largest newspaper, with an average circulation of 402,422 Sunday and 340,260 daily (AAM FAS-FAX March 2013). The _Times_ is produced by the Times Publishing Company, which also publishes TampaBay.com - Tampa Bay's largest local news web site with 2.4 million unique visitors each month[1]. Additionally, the company publishes the free daily _tbt*_, an edition of the _Tampa Bay Times_, _tb-two*_, a free paper written by Tampa Bay area students distributed to students. A website soaring to popularity as people fact-check claims made by political figures, PolitiFact.com, is written by the _Tampa Bay Times staff and has also won a Pulitzer Prize._

[1]Nielsen NetView six-month average for Oct. 2012 –Mar. 2013

The Weekly Challenger, published from their headquarters at 2500 Dr. Martin Luther King, Jr. St. S. and the Florida Sentinel Bulletin gather and present news and information for and about the African American communities of Tampa Bay.

Other community newspapers include _The Suncoast News_, published every Thursday in North Pinellas County. The _St. Petersburg Tribune_ is a special edition of the Tampa Tribune, devoted to news on the West side of the bay.

Creative Loafing covers people, places and politics in St. Petersburg and Tampa on a weekly basis.

Beach Life keeps you abreast of entertainment and activities in St. Petersburg's beach communities.

Gulf Coast Family Newspaper is a handy resource for newcomers, providing lists and locations of pre-schools, attractions, dental and medical resources, family-friendly restaurants, a community events calendar, and children's birthday party ideas.

For your business minded self, keep up with the activities of local business leaders by reading the local publications written for entrepreneurs and corporate executives as well as small business owners and employees on the fast track.

The Business Observer covers business and economic information affecting the Gulf Coast from Tampa Bay south to Naples. I especially like Coffee Talk and never fail to pick up some tidbit of news that helps my Florida-based business. _Tampa Bay Business Journal_ is well read nationwide, perhaps by business owners considering a relocation, as the online edition gets an average of 123,587 unique monthly visitors.

Note that both of these business periodicals publish lists of the top companies in various industries. These are good resources for you when contemplating a job change.

An official "Book of Lists," is published annually by the _Tampa Bay Business Journal_. Be sure to pick up a copy. It is interesting and essential reading for newcomers, even if you are moving to St. Petersburg to retire. Lists of the top banks, home builders, mortgage lenders, and title companies will be helpful in your real estate transactions and when you are settled and ready to play, consult the lists of golf courses, marinas, restaurants, and fund-raising events.

Local Magazines

Grand Magazine: Grandparents in the Burg are so hip, they have a digital magazine. No trees are wasted seeking information such as "60 Cool ways to have fun with your grandchild." Published by St. Petersburg resident Christine Crosby, _Grand Magazine_ is continually updated and invites readers to post their own photos. This magazine is actually published nationwide, but you saw it here first.

St. Pete Magazine: 40,000 copies are direct mailed to every high-income home and business in Tierra Verde, Pinellas Point, Coquina Key, Downtown, Old Northeast, Snell Isle and similar tony neighborhoods. Editorial content is a positive reflection of St. Pete's community, featuring prominent people or exploring St. Pete's colorful history.

Bay Magazine is chock full of in-depth stories about the dining, entertainment, and culture of St. Petersburg , conveniently inserted and delivered to homes in a Sunday edition of the Tampa Bay Times each quarter. It is so beautifully done, you will read it cover to cover!

Florida Trend, also published by the *Tampa Bay Times,* is strictly business, covering the entrepreneurs, government and corporate leaders who champion the economy for the entire state of Florida.

duPont Registry is lovely to look at from the first to the last page. The magazine targets an upscale reader and is distributed to exclusive luxury residential neighborhoods. If you don't get one, then it's probably not for you, if you know what I mean.

Accent On Tampa Bay is a digital magazine that covers arts, entertainment, dining, exciting products and travel, with the local coverage of upcoming events.

Tampa Bay Magazine describes its content as People, Places, Pleasures and Wonders of the Tampa Bay area of Florida and is written for all Tampa/St. Pete audiences, offering the area's best in lifestyle choices from dining to entertainment and beyond since 1986. Contents include art, dining, entertainment, home and garden, fashion, travel and leisure.

Anna Cooke

The New Barker, lets you stay Pup-To-Date on all things dog. Florida's top dog lifestyle magazine. Published by local residents and business owners Steve and Anna Cooke, the magazine is the go-to resource for where to play, dine, shop, vacation and have fun with your dog throughout Florida. See the magazine's online calendar of dog-friendly events updated weekly.

CHAPTER 9

PRACTICAL NOTEBOOK ON MOVING

Transport and Logistics

If your move to St. Petersburg is contracted by a moving company in your previous hometown, you'll be pleased that the major van lines operate in the Tampa Bay area. And, you will appreciate the large number of air conditioned storage units. In fact, these structures are looking pretty posh these days, some offering cold storage for furs, high security storage for jewels and luxury vehicles and climate controlled units for your wine collection. A quick Internet search will yield plenty of options.

Many people are downsizing when they move to Florida. That can be a stressful experience for the entire family. Specialists in helping with those painful logistics are House to Home Relocation. The firm addresses the particular needs of seniors with helpful resources.

An Overseas Move

For those moving to St. Petersburg from overseas, here are some tips:

- Moving by sea can be a long process, taking about six to eight weeks to get all of your household goods to your new St. Petersburg home.

- Moving by air is expensive, but is becomingly increasingly popular because it eliminates the expense of a long hotel stay while your possessions are en route.

- Typically, a small family with an average living and dining room, two bedrooms, a kitchen and miscellaneous books, clothes, dishes and décor, would be enough to fill one standard 20-foot container whose 1,000 cubic feet can hold approximately 6,000 pounds of goods. Larger households may require a 40-foot container.

- Do not pack your own boxes when planning a long-distance move. Leave it to the professionals.

- Ensure that your international moving company is licensed with the Federal Maritime Commission as an Ocean Transportation Intermediary. A reputable mover will be licensed with a tariff and bond.

- Contact the U.S. Embassy to get advice on visas. Personnel may even be able to put you in contact with other expatriates who can share their experiences and provide you with valuable advice.

- Additional insurance is always advisable.

- If you are shipping your car or truck, expect plenty of restrictions, hefty costs, and consider whether or not you are licensed to drive in the U.S. upon your arrival and if your vehicle meets the environmental standards.

- If you have pets, check to see if there are any quarantine requirements.

(Sources: Mover Max, 123 Movers, International Sea & Air Shipping)

Upon the arrival of your household items in the U.S., most, if not all, will be subject to an x-ray procedure. Some containers are randomly selected for a physical inspection, which could result in a delay in customs clearance. Customs clearance will take on average between four and eight days from date of arrival. All non-U.S. citizens must be in the U.S. when the shipment arrives.

Import documentation is checked thoroughly. Make sure you have filled out the proper fields on U.S. Customs Form 3299. Other paperwork that is required is a Supplemental Declaration for unaccompanied personal and household effects and a Power of Attorney if you cannot be present at customs for your shipment to clear. Also, a copy of your work visa and a copy of your passport are needed.

For more information, visit www.internationalmoving.com.

CHAPTER 10

ECONOMIC GROWTH

The Future of St. Petersburg

Chris Steinocher

By CHRIS STEINOCHER, CEO and President of the St. Petersburg Area Chamber of Commerce

The St. Petersburg Area Chamber of Commerce has, in its recent strategic plan, identified economic development as its most important priority over the next three years. Economic development is about creating jobs and enhancing the community and the Chamber's economic development strategy is divided into four parts.

The first part of our economic development strategy is "Start," that is to help make St. Petersburg a place that is friendly to entrepreneurs and eliminates as many barriers to entry for a new business as we can. The main focus of this effort is done through the St. Petersburg Greenhouse, a collaboration of the Chamber and the City to help businesses start and grow. The Greenhouse was created to be the first place that entrepreneurs can come to when they want help starting or growing their business. Capacity-building training programs and classes are offered at the Greenhouse, as well as mentors, counselors, and networking events. You can find more information about the Greenhouse and the programs it offers at www.stpetegreenhouse.org.

The second part of our strategy is "Retain." This is all about ensuring that the companies that we already have here in St. Petersburg are given every opportunity to be successful. The Chamber organizes outreach site-visits to local companies to catch up with them, see how their business is going, and find out what we – as a business community – can do to help them be successful. This is another area that the Chamber's partnership with the City's Economic Development staff pays off. Companies come to know they have access to both public and private resources for help with their business.

The third part of our economic development strategy is "Visit." St. Petersburg has long been a favorite tourist destination for visitors from around the world, and those visitors have a huge economic impact. [Call out] *Not only do visitors impact our economy by the direct purchases they make while in our area, but studies from the Tampa Bay Partnership have found that over 80 percent of businesses that choose to relocate to our area do so because a decision maker discovered us while on vacation.* The Chamber is committed to working with our tourist-facing member businesses to make each visitor's trip to St. Petersburg a positive and memorable one.

The final part of our economic development strategy is "Attract." Community members already know what a great place St. Petersburg is to live, work and play, but it is important for us to share that message with others. The Chamber is undertaking a large public-private partnership effort to enhance our City's visibility in other parts of the nation and world so that we become a go-to destination for companies looking to expand or relocate their operations.

The combination of these four areas is what we feel drives the Economic Development of St. Petersburg.

A growing population, an improving job market and a still undervalued housing market make Tampa Bay one of the nation's 20 best metros to invest in single-family real estate, according to a list compiled by Forbes.com and Local Market Monitor.[1]

[1]Source: Tampa Bay Business Journal

Top Employers, Both Public and Private

Based on number of employees, these are some of the St. Petersburg area's top companies:

Pinellas County School District	15,967
C.W. Bill Young VA Medical Center	4,364
City of St. Petersburg	3,120
Home Shopping Network	2,800
St. Petersburg College	2,697
Raymond James Financial	2,600
Pinellas County Sheriff Office	2,596
Bayfront Medical Center	2,500
Tech Data Corp	2,500
All Children's Hospital	2,300

Source: *Florida Research and Economic Information Database Application*

Headquarters & Branches

Larger corporations are choosing to relocate their corporate headquarters or place a branch of their company in St. Petersburg. Here is a sampling:

Business Name	City	NAICS Description	Local Employees
Home Shopping Network	St. Petersburg	Television Broadcasting	2,800
Raymond James Financial	St. Petersburg	Securities Brokerage	2,600
Bright House Networks	St. Petersburg	Telecommunications Carriers	2,000
Fidelity Information Svc	St. Petersburg	Data Processing & Related Services	1,800
Neilsen Media Research	Oldsmar	All Other Publishers	1,800
Jabil Circuit Inc	St. Petersburg	Other Electronic Component Mfg	1,600
Tech Data Corp	Clearwater	Computer & Software Merchant	2,500
Honeywell Aerospace	Clearwater	Electric Equip & Wiring Merchant	1,500

ThinkDirect Marketing Group	Clearwater	Telemarketing Bureaus & Other Contact Centers	1,000
Ceridian Benefits Services	St. Petersburg	Pension Funds	1,000
Cox Target Media Inc	Largo	Direct Mail Advertising	1,000
Macy's Credit Operations, Inc.	Clearwater	Financial Trans. Processing & Clearing	1,000
DukeEnergy	St. Petersburg	Electric Power Distribution	1,000
Conmed Linvatec	Largo	Surgical & Medical Instrument Mfg	970
Transamerica Life Insurance	St. Petersburg	Insurance Agencies & Brokerages	900
Franklin Templeton Invest.	St. Petersburg	Misc Intermediation	900
PSCU Financial Svc Inc	St. Petersburg	Financial Trans. Processing & Clearing	850
Regions Bank	Clearwater	Commercial Banking	850

Raytheon Co	Seminole	Engineering Services	800
Baxter Healthcare Mfg	Largo	Medical Equip Merchant	700

Why Companies Locate in St. Petersburg

The reasons people move here as residents are the very same reasons businesses want to relocate here. St. Petersburg's economic climate is a perfect place for your business to bloom. The beautiful weather and surroundings that we are privileged to have provides inspiration, prompts creativity, and ensures a happier work force. Entrepreneurs, scientists, artists, musicians, professionals and students coexist due to the prolific opportunities and relationship building. When there aren't any snow storms and freezing temperatures to keep people indoors, it increases momentum for business ventures and connects professionals. This validation within the entrepreneurial scene creates a sense of accountability that is unique to St. Petersburg. The New York Times named St. Petersburg as one of the top 52 places to go giving a nod to the small businesses in St. Petersburg. Reinvention and renovation are keys to our small business growth.

Entrepreneurial Pursuits

"The St. Petersburg Chamber of Commerce offers many programs and events beneficial to all types of businesses and entrepreneurs from young start-ups to those reinventing themselves post-retirement," says Chris Steinocher, CEO and President of the St. Petersburg Area Chamber of Commerce. *"Industrial parks in the area are goldmines for job creation. These existing buildings can be transformed into manufacturing plants or other businesses at low cost with high return while creating new employment opportunities."* As more neighborhoods and condominiums fill with newcomers who decide St. Petersburg is a perfect place to live, work and play, the economy grows. The impact each person makes creates an overwhelming sense of pride throughout all avenues of business.

City leaders like Steinocher care about what they can do for businesses and how they can continue to attract economic development into the future.

Employment Market

St. Petersburg has experienced extensive growth that continues to improve the job market. The health corridor in downtown St. Petersburg boasts the best medical facilities in the area, and welcomed John's Hopkins School of Medicine to the Bayfront health district on 6ᵗʰ Avenue South. These additions brought new, lasting employment opportunities.

Just down the street and around the corner is one of the most successful Marine Science and Health programs in the nation at the University of South Florida. Students experience engaged learning in the best environment with support from organizations like the National Oceanic and Atmospheric Administration (NOAA), and these programs plan to grow as anchors in the community. The manufacturing industry has begun to call St. Petersburg home again, and brought higher paying jobs to the region.

Computer science and technology is a booming job market in the area. St. Petersburg has become an appealing alternative to Silicon Valley in the tech world because of the low cost of building a business and the local demand for developers. These positions lower the average age of the City's population. Well-educated professionals are eager to see what benefits the city can reap from hard work and dedication. In only a short time, St. Petersburg has changed and the market is expected to continue the upward trend.

Here are the top 25 highest paying jobs in Pinellas County:

Occupation Title	2012 Annual Median Level Wage
Chief Executives	$169,906.63
Family and General Practitioners	$163,978.26
Dentists, General	$142,865.99
Pharmacists	$131,063.58
Computer and Information Systems Managers	$130,675.44
Engineering Managers	$118,305.65
Transportation, Storage, and Distribution Managers	$118,149.57
Sales Managers	$113,927.35
Financial Managers	$110,183.57
Human Resources Managers, All Other	$108,690.14
Marketing Managers	$103,359.07
Securities, Commodities, and Financial Services Sales Agents	$101,395.69
Civil Engineers	$97,024.71
Medical and Health Services Managers	$96,992.59
Veterinarians	$96,234.22

Occupation Title	2012 Annual Median Level Wage
Natural Sciences Managers	$94,599.43
Industrial Production Managers	$93,051.93
Purchasing Managers	$92,919.31
Administrative Services Managers	$92,445.99
Managers, All Other	$92,270.53
Lawyers	$92,128.15
First-Line Supervisors/Managers of Fire Fighting and Prevention Workers	$89,922.45
Architects, Except Landscape and Naval	$88,306.94
Physical Therapists	$88,181.81
General and Operations Managers	$88,085.04

[1]FloridaTaxWatch.org May 2012

[2]EmployFlorida.com 2012

[3]EmployFlorida.com as of February 27, 2013

CONCLUSION

There's plenty to love about Saint Pete!

- Low cost of living

- Waterfront homes

- Proximity to wildlife

- Accessible beaches

- Great healthcare

- Friendly people

- Unlimited outdoor fun

- Dedicated parks and preserves

- Sports teams and entertainment

- Cultural activities

- Wonderful weather

- Booming business community

Clearly by now, you realize that St. Pete is much more than a retirement destination. It is ideal for seniors and anyone smart enough to be enjoying the Florida lifestyle now, reaping the benefits of no state income tax, lower property taxes and energy costs, and more affordable housing.

But, why wait until retirement, when you could be thriving in St. Pete right now?

Professionals are discovering lots of opportunities with the top companies mentioned earlier in this book. Firms are expanding their operations and entrepreneurs are bringing new options to the area, providing jobs for eager college grads or experienced employees. Growing families are finding affordable housing, excellent healthcare, and good schools. Active adults are enjoying plenty of activities and attractions to meet their busy lifestyles.

Most importantly, everyone is finding a quality of life here that many didn't believe they could actually enjoy until their golden years. The drive into work or school is not hindered by traffic jams and long commutes. And at the end of the day, you can catch a sunset on the beach.

Whether you are escaping cold weather or considering this area as a place to relocate your corporate headquarters, be sure to give St. Pete very careful consideration.

Multi-generation families and business owners here have known all along what a great place it is to live, to work, and to play. Compared to other cities of its age, St. Petersburg is unspoiled and beautiful year round. It is a credit to those long time residents who serve in local government and as community leaders working to *keep* St. Pete unspoiled and beautiful.

"The Burg" is getting lots of positive nationwide attention lately. The secret is out and you are now in the know. If you've read this far, you likely don't need much more incentive to pack your belongings and move to St. Petersburg. You will be warmly welcomed.

IMPORTANT PHONE NUMBERS AND WEBSITE LINKS

City of St. Petersburg Government
www.stpete.org
(727) 893-7111

St. Petersburg Chamber of Commerce
www.stpete.com
(727) 821-4069

Pinellas County Information
www.pinellascounty.org

Pinellas County Property Appraiser
www.pcpao.org/
(727) 464-3207

Pinellas County Realtor Organization
www.pinellasrealtor.org
(727) 347-7655

Pinellas County Economic Development
www.pced.org

Pinellas County Dental Association
www.smilepinellas.com/Directory/index.htm
(727) 342-0374

Driver's Licenses
www.dmvflorida.org/pinellas.shtml
(727) 464-7777

Fishing Licenses
www.myfwc.com
(888) 347-4356

Marriage Licenses
www.pinellasclerk.org/aspinclude2/ASPInclude.
asp?pageName=marriage.htm
(727) 464-4700

Social Security
www.socialsecurityofficelocation.net/st-petersburg-florida-social-
security-office-so1624
(800) 772-1213

Tax Collector
www.taxcollect.com
(727) 464-7777

Vehicle Registration
www.dmvflorida.org/car-registration.shtml
(727) 464-7777

Voter Registration
www.votepinellas.com/?id=2
(727) 464-8683

Pinellas County Public Schools
www.pcsb.org
(727) 588-6000

Pinellas County Parks
www.pinellascounty.org/park/default.htm
(727) 582-2100

Boat Registration
www.taxcollect.com/vessels-2
(727) 464-7777

Duke Energy
www.progress-energy.com/florida/support/contact-us/index.page
(727) 443-2641

TECO (Gas)
www.peoplesgas.com/contact
(727) 826-3333

Brighthouse (Cable)
www.brighthouse.com/tampa-bay/default
(888) 289-8988

Verizon (Telephone)
www.verizon.com
(800) 483-3000

Pinellas County Water & Sewer
www.pinellascounty.org/resident/watersewer.htm
(727) 464-3000

City of St. Petersburg Water & Sewer
www.stpete.org/water
(727) 893-7261

City of St. Petersburg Garbage Collection
www.stpete.org/sanitation/residential_collection
(727) 893-7334

Pinellas County Garbage Collection
www.pinellascounty.org/resident/trash.htm
(727) 464-3000

Bus Services

Pinellas County Transit Authority
www.psta.net/index.php#
(727) 540-1800

Business Assistance

SCORE
www.pinellascounty.score.org
(727) 532-6800

Occupational Licensing
www.pinellascounty.org/occupational_licenses.htm
(727) 464-3000

Hospitals

All Children's Hospital
www.allkids.org
(727) 898-7451

St. Anthony's Hospital
www.stanthonys.com
(727) 825-1100

Bayfront Health St. Petersburg
www.bayfront.com
(727) 823-1234

St. Petersburg General Hospital
www.stpetegeneral.com
(727) 384-1414

Palms of Pasadena Hospital
www.palmspasadena.com
(727) 381-1000

Edward White Hospital
www.edwardwhitehospital.com
(727) 323-1111

Northside Hospital
www.northsidehospital.com
(727) 521-4411

Largo Medical Center
www.largomedical.com
(727) 588-5200

Ambulatory Surgery Center of Tampa
www.tampaambulatory.com
(813) 977-8550

Memorial Hospital of Tampa
www.memorialhospitaltampa.com
(813) 873-6400

Tampa Eye and Specialty Surgery Center
www.tampaeyesurgery.com
(813) 870-6330

C.W. Bill Young VA Medical Center
www.baypines.va.gov
(727) 398-6661

Police Non-Emergency

Pinellas County Sheriff's Office
www.pcsoweb.com
(727) 582-6200

St. Petersburg Police Department
www.stpete.org/police
(727) 893-7780

Fire Non-Emergency

Pinellas County Fire Administration
www.pinellascounty.org/publicsafety/fire_admin.htm
(727) 582-2437

St. Petersburg Fire and Rescue
www.stpete.org/fire
(727) 893-7694

ACKNOWLEDGEMENTS

All of the kind help I received while researching this book is further testament to how friendly the people are in St. Petersburg. Early encouragement from my wonderfully supportive family and friends like Diana Murray, helped me to say, "Yes," when publisher Newt Barrett invited me to take on this challenge and I am grateful for his professional advice and friendship. *Moving to St. Petersburg: The Un-Tourist Guide* and our actual relocation to this city would not be possible without the kind understanding and diligent research provided by my best friend and husband Mike Dobyns. He spent hours proofing drafts, as did my inspirational friend and colleague Alysia Shivers, author of *Moving to Naples*, the first book of Voyager Media Inc.'s promising series. Special thanks to the talented Mary Lou Jansen, author of *Moving to Tampa: The Un-Tourist Guide,* who compared notes and swapped content as we wrote our books at the same time.

So many people recommended former St. Petersburg Mayor Rick Baker as a resource. I am grateful to him and his assistant Emily Sitzberger at The Edwards Group for writing the Foreword to *Moving to St. Petersburg: The Un-Tourist Guide.*

Thank you to those who took my calls and spent time talking about St. Petersburg, especially historians Jon Wilson and Gwen Reese, generous neighbors Tom and Katy Cleary, Tim and Marianne Skarupa, John Hislop, and our Realtor and friend Betty Youmans, who found our home in Treasure Island. I am grateful to have attended a Press Club talk by *Tampa Bay Times* columnist Jeff Klinkenberg that taught me how to find my voice. Excellent professors at Eckerd College and University of South Florida laid the groundwork and I will always be grateful to the former St. Petersburg Times editors (Andy Barnes, Mike Moscardini, Robert Jenkins, Helen Huntley, Ruth Gray and other forgotten names) who encouraged me to write when I was an intern. Former *St. Petersburg Times* writer Jon Wilson took the time to review the manuscript and provided invaluable fact-checking for which I am very grateful.

St. Petersburg has many other outstanding professional communicators who contributed their words and photography to this book, including: Robert Danielson, City of St. Petersburg; Mary Burrell, Pinellas County Communications; Stacey L. Swank, Pinellas County Economic Development; Leroy Bridges, St. Petersburg/Clearwater Area Convention & Visitors Bureau; Jounice L. Nealy-Brown, *Tampa Bay Times*; Sean Kennedy, Greenhouse Manager/Economic Development Coordinator, Kristina Alspaw, Visitor Development & Promotion Coordinator and ever smiling Annie Poling at St. Petersburg Area Chamber of Commerce; Michael Atwell, Clearwater Marine Aquarium; Susan Strawbridge, Homosassa Springs Wildlife State Park; Jennifer M. Johnson, Florida Fish & Wildlife Conservation Commission; Tom Scherberger, University of South Florida St. Petersburg; Susan Bass, Big Cat Rescue; Jeff Jensen, City of Treasure Island; Debra McKell, HCA West Florida Division; Cassie Lovett, Imagine Communications, Anna Cooke, *The New Barker Magazine*; Jonni Watts, St. Pete/Clearwater Film Commission; Robin O. Felix, Southwest Florida Water Management District; Jeff Abbaticchio, Loews Don CeSar Hotel; Holly Dennis, American Society of Interior Designers Florida West Coast; Carla A. Mitchell and Len Ciecieznski, Pinellas Citizen University; and Briant Marsh and Sharon Van Rite on behalf of Vinoy Renaissance St. Petersburg Resort & Golf Club.

Photographs were kindly provided by professional photographers Gareth Rockliffe, Jan Soderquist, David Schrichte and Laura Osteen, as well as Tim Marusarz, Kelly Franckowiak, Karen Quilty and Gail Eggeman. Thank you Carli Todd, Erik Ruiz and Skip Milos with the Tampa Bay Rays.

Pages of this book would not have been possible without the patience and efficiency of Lynn Cissna, Admin Rockstar at the St. Petersburg Area Chamber of Commerce and her boss, the Chamber's President and CEO Chris Steinocher who with his talented team contributed information about the economy in St. Petersburg.

My warmest appreciation goes to my business partners and friends Mary Jane Kolassa and John M. Williams who kept their talented eyes on AboveWater Public Relations during this project and contributed to the research. Thanks, Mom, for amassing helpful newspaper clips and magazines, for being my fact checker, and for recommending Casey's Cookies as the perfect corporate gift. Thank you, too, for agreeing with Dad to move here so we could grow up across the street from the Gulf of Mexico and meet lifelong friends like Joy and Gary Ismet, the Youmans, and the McNulty's.

ABOUT THE AUTHOR

Soderquist Photography

You *can* go home again and that's what author Cindy Dobyns has done. When home recalls memories of wiggling your toes in the powdery sand beaches of St. Petersburg, Florida who can resist? Her forward-thinking father decided it was time to leave chilly Chicago and piled four kids into the Oldsmobile heading south to seek fortune in Treasure Island, hoping it would be a lifestyle all would enjoy. Warm and friendly St. Petersburg turned out to be the best place to raise children.

Cindy attended Eckerd College and graduated from the University of South Florida with a degree in Mass Communications. Though college and careers scattered the siblings, brother Danny, today a cheerful UPS driver, never left his St. Petersburg zip code. The family chides him, but they are secretly jealous. Cindy set a goal to return to St. Petersburg some day.

She founded AboveWater Public Relations and Marketing, LLC in Naples, Florida after a whirlwind career first in magazine publishing, then in the hospitality industry that took her from Florida to New York and New Jersey to Washington, D.C. One snowy New Year's Eve, she and her husband Mike vowed to return to Florida. That was more than a decade ago, when both found jobs at hotels in Southwest Florida and two years later, opened AboveWater to essentially keep their own heads above water. The marketing firm has grown to serve clients nationwide from offices in Naples, New Smyrna Beach, and Tampa. Cindy happily flies to northern cities to meet with news media and clients, but she would never want to live there, now that she calls St. Petersburg home again.

Made in the USA
Lexington, KY
14 December 2015